Is God to Blame?

Reconciling Suffering with a Good God

Tom Peers

Ragamuffin Publishing Company - Portland, Maine
www.ragamuffinpublishing.com
tom@ragamuffinpublishing.com

Is God to Blame?/ Tom Peers. -- 1st ed.
ISBN-10: 0-9970998-0-1   ISBN-13: 978-0-9970998-0-5

Table of Contents

Introduction

2 Corinthians 1:3,4

> *Blessed be the God and Father of our Lord Jesus Christ, the Father of mercies and God of all comfort, who comforts us in all our affliction so that we will be able to comfort those who are in any affliction with the comfort with which we ourselves are comforted by God.*

I don't believe God causes our affliction and then comforts us while we're in it. That seems like twisted logic to me.

Additionally, I don't believe that kind of thinking lines up with God's character of love, mercy and compassion as revealed in Scripture or what we see in the life of Jesus Christ. And that is precisely what this book is about.

There are numerous books on the topic of suffering. I have read many of them, and although my heart resonated with the comfort they offered to those suffering, my head and intellect rejected many of their arguments. I just couldn't reconcile what they were saying with the God of the Bible that I was reading about, especially as observed in the life of Jesus Christ in the New Testament.

And so, I have attempted here to pen another view of suffering to help people reconcile suffering with a good God. This book, therefore, is what is called in philosophy, a *theodicy*. A theodicy is a vindication of the goodness of God in light of the existence of evil and suffering. It basically is a defense of God and His goodness by addressing the problem of evil.

I will argue for the case that God is good and not the author of mankind's suffering. Scripture is clear about the sources of evil and suffering, and I will attempt to elucidate these points the best I can. I hope, in the very least, I have added something important to the discussion and have caused people to consider a different paradigm on the subject.

If you are not a theist (one who believes in God) or Christian, I would suggest you read *Part 1 - Laying a Foundation*, skip Part 2 and then move on to *Part 3 - Ten Reasons for Suffering*. The reason is, Part 2 is geared toward Christians who have been taught certain things in church or elsewhere that have contributed to some theology that needs adjusting. Of course, even Part 3 is written from a Christian standpoint, but I believe an atheist or agnostic will still find Part 3 helpful.

If you are a Christian, I invite you, at least temporarily while reading the book, to lay aside your preconceived thinking on certain doctrines and theology that you've picked up along the way. I plan to challenge some of that theology, and, in order to give this a fair shot, it will take being open-minded. Admittedly, this is easier said than done. But if you will just try to stay open, I believe you will find this book enlightening. I encourage you to be a good "Berean".

Acts 17:11

> The people of Berea were more **open-minded** than those in Thessalonica, and they listened eagerly to Paul's message. They **searched the Scriptures** day after day **to see if Paul and Silas were teaching the truth.** (NLT)

I apologize up front for this book being more academic than emotive in tone and tenor. Although I have great compassion and empathy for those who are suffering, lost loved ones, have family members with permanent disabilities, or who grieve, as I do, when watching the aftermath of natural disasters and calamities; the purpose of this book is more aimed at the head than the heart. My intent is to present a reasoned response to the existence of suffering in view of God's goodness.

For the sake of brevity, I don't share examples or real life stories of people who have suffered and struggled with the theology that God causes suffering. And I don't try to formulate truth based on people's experiences. I base spiritual truth on just one thing, God's Word.

John 17:17

> Sanctify them in the truth; **Your word is truth**.

If our experience doesn't align with the truth of Scripture, we need to reevaluate it to ascertain how we might be misinterpreting that experience. This is the essence of what the Apostle Paul said.

Galatians 1:8

> *But even if we, or an angel from heaven, should preach to you a gospel contrary to what we have preached to you, he is to be accursed!*

Experience can anecdotally affirm spiritual truth, but it doesn't determine it.

Additionally, I don't tease out arguments to their exhaustive conclusions. I have intentionally tried to be brief and to the point hoping this will allow for a quick yet adequate treatment of this subject.

Part 1

Laying a Foundation

CHAPTER 1

The Problem

In a recent Facebook conversation with an atheist about God's existence, a person said to me:

Honestly, if I'm wrong and he DOES exist, he will have an EARFUL as I have a lot of shit to discuss with him. His supposed 'all powerful yet all loving' gig isn't jiving as I could be a better god if I had those types of powers - as far as I'm concerned if he's truly all powerful he's also cruel because no all-loving and all-powerful being would allow the suffering and deaths of billions of innocent children amongst other things. ... There's zero love in that."

Georg Büchner (1813-1837), a German poet, playwright, and natural scientist, once said, "Suffering is the rock of atheism."[1] In other words, the existence of suffering is the atheists' ultimate trump card when trying to disprove God's existence. It is a natural human reaction to the evil and suffering we experience or witness here on earth to, even subconsciously, wonder, "If there is a God, why would He allow all this suffering?"

In the final chapter of John Stott's classic work *The Cross of Christ*, the book closes with a chapter entitled, *Suffering and Glory*. Stott says:

> *The fact of suffering undoubtedly constitutes the single greatest challenge to the Christian faith.[2]*

The thought of suffering and a good God is upsetting. It's been upsetting people for thousands of years. In the book of Job, a man by the name of Job (pronounced *Jōb*) struggled with major-league suffering and God's alleged participation in it. Believing that God was actively behind his suffering, Job exclaims to Him:

Job 7:19, 20

> *Will you never look away from me, or let me alone even for an instant? If I have sinned, what have I done to you, you who sees everything we do? Why have you made me your target? Have I become a burden to you?*

In actuality, it was not God doing this to Job, it was Satan.

Job 2:7

> *So Satan went out from the presence of the Lord and afflicted Job.*

The point here is that the problem of evil and suffering has been plaguing mankind's thoughts for millennia.

There are three categories of evil:

1. **Natural evil**—pain, sickness, disease, disabilities, earthquakes, floods, tornadoes, accidents, calamities, viruses and plagues.

2. **Supernatural evil**—evil done directly from Satan and evil spirits.

3. **Moral evil**—man's inhumanity to man, evil decisions and actions; murder, genocide, theft and domination.

Even in insurance policies, natural evil like floods, earthquakes or tornadoes are called "acts of God." In the movie, *The Witches of Eastwick*, Jack Nicholson's character, Daryl Van Horne, picks up on this:

When we make mistakes, they call it evil. When God makes mistakes, they call it Nature!³

This shows that most people ascribe the cause of evil to God Himself.

To say that God permits evil in the world may not be pleasing to the ear. But if He is held responsible for the good, it follows that He has to be responsible for the evil too.⁴

- Mahatma Gandhi

God responsible for the evil in the world? May it never be!

Mankind has been struggling with reconciling evil and suffering with the goodness of God for a long time. The Greek philosopher, Epicurus (341-270 BC), framed it this way:

Is God willing to prevent evil, but not able? Then he is not omnipotent.

Is he able, but not willing? Then he is malevolent.

Is he both able and willing? Then whence cometh evil?

Is he neither able nor willing? Then why call him God?⁵

Admittedly, that's a powerful argument. Deficient, but powerful.

To put it another way, if God is all-good and all-loving, and evil happens, then He must not be powerful enough to stop it. If God is powerful enough to stop it and doesn't, then He must not be all-good and loving. The natural default conclusion is, there is no God.

Sometimes it's put as a *syllogism*. A syllogism is comprised of two givens resulting in a conclusion. It would look like this:

1. If God exists, God would not allow evil.

2. Evil exists.

3. Therefore, God does not exist.

This logic has allegedly affected two celebrities, both from CNN, Larry King⁶ and Ted Turner⁷. Both gentlemen allegedly do not believe in God for this very reason. The problem of the concurrent existence of God and evil/suffering has troubled every human being, theist and atheist alike.

When evil happens, people shake their fist at God in accusation as if He was the one that caused it.

In December 2004, there was a tsunami in Indonesia and Southeast Asia that killed over a quarter of a million people. That is hard for our minds to comprehend. Two months later there was an article in the magazine, *The Progressive*, by Barbara Ehrenreich called, *God Owes Us an Apology*, where she stated:

> *If God cares about our puny species, then disasters prove that he is not all-powerful; and if he is all-powerful, then clearly he doesn't give a damn.*[8]

Ouch.

So how do we reconcile evil and suffering with a God who is both all-good and all-powerful? There are answers to this troublesome question, and that's what this book is about. I want to give you ten reasons why bad things happen to people; why evil and suffering are allowed to exist. But first, the next chapters here in Part 1 serve as an introduction.

CHAPTER 2

But God Allowed It

I want to address right off the bat the "but God allowed it" response to evil and suffering. What's implicit in this response is that God caused it and did so for a reason, the "everything happens for a reason" line of thinking (more on this in Chapter 10).

In other words, not only did God allow this evil to occur, but He was actually the one who caused it to happen for His own strategic purposes. The thinking goes like this:

It happened, so God allowed it.

If God allowed it, He caused it.

If He caused it, He did so for a divine purpose.

If you adhere to reformed theology and Calvinism, this is exactly how you think. But I don't embrace reformed theology or Calvinism, so I don't buy the argument. Calvinists believe this argument because God is "sovereign", which to them means that everything that happens here on earth was caused by God and is therefore His will. In this case, when suffering something bad, the only thing one can do is be thankful when it's over.

It's like the predestinationalist who fell down the stairs at his house one morning. At the bottom of the stairs, he got up, shook his head and said, "Boy, I'm glad that's over!" You see, that's about all you can do if you're a Calvinist.

If you believe God is the one bringing suffering into your life, you'll just roll over and accept it. It's like a grizzly bear attack, you roll over and play dead until the attack is over. If God's the grizzly bear on attack, you'll do the same thing. But my position is that God is NOT behind your suffering.

It's not the purpose or scope of this book to treat Calvinism theology and show why I believe it to be defective. I go into more detail about this in my book *Lord and Savior.*[9] If one adheres to Calvinism, it makes the answer to suffering and evil quite simple: "God did it for some transcendent reason and we shouldn't question why. End of argument, nothing else to talk about, nothing to see here so move along." Except this doesn't help people and additionally, it besmirches the character of God. Neither are acceptable to me.

The "God allowed it" answer to suffering just doesn't cut it. Just because God allowed something to happen doesn't mean He wanted it to happen. Let's think through the ramifications of such thinking.

- God allowed Lucifer to rebel against God and take a third of the angels with him. Does that mean that it was God's will for Lucifer and company to rebel against Him? I hardly think so.
- God allowed Adam & Eve to sin, does that mean it was His will?
- God allowed Israel to grumble and complain resulting in them wandering the desert for 40 years instead of going directly into the promised land. Was it His will that they grumble, complain and rebel?
- God allowed Israel to worship a golden calf, was it His will?
- God allowed 6 million Jews to be exterminated during the Holocaust, was it His will?
- In 1994, God allowed Susan Smith to strap her two young sons (three-year old Michael and fourteen-month old Alexander) into their car seats, put the car in drive, get out, and allow the car to drive into John D. Long Lake, near Union, South Carolina, drowning them. Does that mean it was His will that Susan do that?

We could go on and on with examples because scripture and life in general are replete with them.

This touches on a critical point ... man's free will. God desired His creation to love Him freely. He didn't want a world of robots, expressing love for Him but being compelled to do so with no choice of their own. Forced "love" is rape, which is no love at all, it's the opposite of genuine love. So God created mankind with free will.

The drawback to free will is—just like man can choose to love and show compassion, he is also free to choose to hate and cause suffering. And God, being the Alpha and Omega, the beginning and the end (Revelation 1:8 and 22:13), because He is omniscient (all-knowing), and therefore knowing that man was going to blow it by sinning in the Garden of Eden, still thought this tradeoff was worth it.

People ask, "Well, if He knew they would sin, why did He even go through with this plan?" The answer is—because even knowing they'd blow it, in the very end, at the consummation of the ages, in the final state of heaven on a newly created earth, God would have billions and billions of His children who freely chose to love and follow Him, and enjoy Him and His creation forever. So in the end, it was worth it.

The point...when you have free will, you have the possibility of choosing wrong, opening the door for evil and subsequent suffering.

The principle I'm driving at here is this:

*Just because God allowed it **doesn't** mean it was His will!*

So I think it's time we dispense with this silly argument, "Well, it happened, so God allowed it." I have news for us, and this is deeply profound...anything that happens here on earth, God obviously allowed! So what? God will allow you to rob First National Bank, but that doesn't mean it's His will.

And yet, this is exactly the response most Christians have to evil and suffering. In some Bible study or discussion group, one person will recount the terrible things that happened to Sister Broomhilda Hucklemeister. There will be a pause, and then someone will say, "Well, yes, but God allowed it," and everyone present will nod their heads in agreement. But you haven't said anything intelligent when you say, "God allowed it." Obviously He did.

When I was in the Air Force, stationed in southern Turkey, I witnessed first-hand how Muslim beliefs affected their behavior. These drivers, including taxi drivers, would ignore red lights and stop signs and just blow on through them with barely a glance. It was terrifying! Eventually I inquired why they did that. The answer was, "If it's the will of Allah, we'll be safe, and if it's not, we won't."

I thought this was nuts. Then I came back to the U.S. fifteen months later and heard Christians saying the exact same thing! If you weren't healed, it wasn't the will of God. If you were healed, it was the will of God. If your prayers were answered, it was God's will. If your prayers weren't answered, well, I guess it wasn't God's will. Anything that happened or didn't happen, was God's will!

Just because God allowed something doesn't mean He caused it or wanted it to happen. We must therefore jettison this argument because...it is, in actuality, no substantive argument at all.

CHAPTER 3

No God–No Evil

As stated earlier, the most prominent argument against God's existence is the reality of evil and human suffering. How could there possibly be an all-loving God with the reality of this much suffering in the world? But here the atheist finds himself in a contradiction. You see:

If there is no God, there is no evil!

So in reality, the atheist has nothing to complain about. Let me explain.

If there is no God, the existence of the universe, earth, animals, and you and me can only best be explained by what is called "scientific materialism." This is based on Darwinian evolution, which states that everything started from some pond scum or primordial soup, evolved into animals, and then eventually into you and me. We call this, "From goo to you by way of the zoo."

But we must dig deeper here, contemplating the ramifications of our thinking. Most people don't think deeply about the implications of their own beliefs.

If everything was originally created from dead, non-thinking molecules (and by the way, where did those molecules come from?), and Darwin's process of natural selection kicked in, then everything is based on survival of the fittest, with no objective moral imperative other than "do what you have to do to survive, be happy and propagate."

If there is no God, then there is no Lawgiver, and therefore no laws. Consequently, no objective standard of morality exists, and therefore no standard of right and wrong, good or evil.

One may choose (actually a diehard materialist will say they didn't choose, they did only what was programmed in their DNA) to do some compassionate or benevolent act for an altruistic purpose, but that's only THEIR preference. By the same token, I could choose to take an action that helps me get ahead (survival of the fittest), say lie, steal, or even murder, and that would be MY preference, which you must EQUALLY accept.

The great Russian novelist, journalist and philosopher, Fyodor Dostoyevsky (1821-1881) said:

If God does not exist, then everything is permitted.[10]

And that's spot on.

Materialists believe that we are comprised only of matter and energy. Therefore, our actions are entirely determined by that matter and energy. A genuine materialist (atheist) believes that we are programmed to behave the way we do and that free will is simply an illusion. Not sure atheists of the Darwinian evolution persuasion believe this? Listen to eminent scholars who teach this position.

"Human free will is nonexistent. ... Free will is a disastrous and mean social myth."[11]

– William Provine (Evolutionary biologist, Professor of History of Biology, Cornell University).

If there is no God, then our DNA drives all behavior, and if that is true, then there is no good and evil, just programmed behavior untethered from volition (free will). A human can kill someone who is in their way to succeed just like the cheetah in Africa can kill another cheetah who he feels is a threat to his survival. It's survival of the fittest. You can't blame the cheetah, and you can't blame the poor person who kills a rich person in order to acquire their assets so they can survive and thrive in life. After all, the materialist says it's all in our genes to survive in this way.

"Morality ... is merely an adaptation put in place to further our reproductive end. ... In an important sense, ethics as we understand it is an illusion fobbed off on us by our genes to get us to cooperate."[12]

– Michael Ruse and E.O. Wilson

If there is no objective morality anchored in God, then the only thing we're left with are personal preferences.

If we're products of pond scum that evolved, then we act as we're programmed to act, and right and wrong is nonexistent. Evolutionary biologist Richard Dawkins, of Oxford University, a staunch atheist and predominant advocate for the Neo-Darwinism movement, admits this inevitable product of the materialist worldview in his book *River Out of Eden: A Darwinian View of Life*:

> *In a universe of electrons and selfish genes, blind physical forces and genetic replication, some people are going to get hurt, other people are going to get lucky, and you won't find any rhyme or reason in it, nor any justice. The universe that we observe has precisely the properties we should expect if there is, at bottom, no design, no purpose, no evil, no good, nothing but pitiless indifference. ... DNA neither knows nor cares. DNA just is, and we dance to its music.[13]*

So with scientific materialists (atheists), there is no real free will. Author Frank Turek, in his book *Stealing from God*, shows how atheists must actually steal from God in order to prove that He doesn't exist. They have to steal objective morality from God in order to make the case that if there truly was a God, He would put an end to evil and suffering.

> *In order to hold people morally responsible for their actions, atheists need to steal free will and morality from God.[14]*

Dr. Lance Waldie, in his book, *A Christian Apologetic for Christian Apologists*, tells the story of Cornelius Van Til, who one time observed a little girl sitting in her father's lap and slapping him.

> *His observation of the event was that the girl had to be sitting in her father's lap to have the capability to slap him. In the same way, the atheist must exist in God's world and assume His existence in order to attempt to disprove His existence.[15]*

He likened that observation to atheists. In reality, Atheists must have God pull them up on His lap in order to slap Him so they can disprove His existence. They need God to disprove God, which is faulty thinking.

Again, one can choose to do what they feel is good, but it has equal weight to someone else who chooses the opposite. No complaining, no moralizing.

The inevitable result of Darwinian evolution is moral relativism. Moral relativism says that morality is relative only to an individual's preference and cannot be applied to everyone else. Ethical norms are not binding on the whole of humanity. So atheists have no right to complain about evil or suffering because those things only make sense if there's a God, a God who gives to mankind objective moral standards, thereby defining what good and evil are in the first place.

In the book by Francis Beckwith and Greg Koukl, *Relativism: Feet Firmly Planted in Mid-Air*, the authors state:

> *Relativists can't accuse others of wrongdoing. That is because if you believe morality is a matter of personal preference, or definition, then you surrender the possibility about making moral judgments about others' actions. A consistent relativist, one who believes there is no ultimate standard of right and wrong, could not with integrity favor abortion or oppose abortion, or oppose racism.*[16]

In fact, atheists and moral relativists have eight things they can't do.

Moral relativists can't: [17]
1. Accuse others of wrong-doing.
2. Complain about being mistreated.
3. Place blame or accept praise.
4. Make charges of unfairness or injustice.
5. Improve their morality.
6. Hold meaningful moral discussions about what one "should do."
7. Say it's wrong to be intolerant.
8. Complain about the problem of evil.

Why? Because without God there is no right, wrong, good, evil, or suffering. There only is...what is.

Additionally, a question to ask the atheist is about his willingness to accept God's intervention IF God, in fact, did exist. A conversation might sound like this:

Me: You're angry because if there was a God, He certainly would intervene to stop evil and suffering, right?

Atheist: Correct!

Me: So if there was a God, would you allow Him to intervene in YOUR life to prevent you from experiencing evil and suffering?

Atheist: Of course I would.

Me: So you would willingly follow God's commandments to not commit fornication, adultery, look at pornography, do drugs, get drunk, cheat people, lust after people, take His name in vain, or acquire way more possessions than you need and then become a follower of Jesus Christ?

Atheist: Well, now wait a minute, no, I don't want Him butting in and raining on my parade. It's my life, stay out.

And this would unveil the great hypocrisy and contradiction of the atheist. Here's the contradiction:

I'm angry that You don't intervene!

Wait, I don't want You to intervene!

Well, guess what? You can't have it both ways!

In the book, *The Atheist's Fatal Flaw - Exposing Conflicting Beliefs*, by Normal L. Geisler and Daniel J. McCoy, the authors identify this contradiction:

The atheist thinks God ought to fix the problem of moral evil. However, the atheist also values human autonomy, a value that helps us understand why the atheist rejects any interventions into the problem of moral evil that would threaten that autonomy.[18]

If you want God to intervene to stop evil and suffering, then you would have to be willing for Him to tell you to stop certain behaviors that result in evil and suffering! But the atheist doesn't want to allow this. Jesus touched on a possible reason for this.

John 3:19-20

> *This is the judgment, that the Light has come into the world, and* **men loved the darkness rather than the Light, for their deeds were evil**. *For everyone who does evil hates the Light, and does not come to the Light* **for fear that his deeds will be exposed.**

Some people's sentiment is, "I want the Light (God) to break into planet earth in order to stop all the suffering, but at the same time, leave me alone." Sorry, it doesn't work that way. So if there's no God, there's no evil, so the atheist has nothing to complain about if they want to remain coherent with their own world view. But even the atheist knows morality is good, both for him and society. Voltaire said:

> *If God did not exist, we should have to invent him.*[19]

Chapter 4

Is God Always in Control?

When I was kid, I remember singing "He's got the whole world in His hands, He's got the whole wide world in His hands, He's got the whole world in His hands, He's got the whole world in His hands."

The implication is that everything that happens here on earth is controlled by God. If that's true, He's got it in quite a mess.

Is everything that happens to you from God? Is everything that happens on earth God's will? Are God's plans always accomplished here on earth?

If you say yes, then what you're saying is that it was God's will that little babies and children were run over and killed by an Islamic terrorist in Nice, France on July 14, 2016.

If you believe everything that happens on earth is God's will, then you believe it was God's will December 26, 2004 that over 250,000 people (men, women, children, babies) died in a Tsunami in Indonesia and Thailand.

If you believe everything that happens on earth is God's will, then you must believe that the Rwandan genocide of 1994 with the murders of 800,000 people was ordained by God.

So is God always in control? Do we have free will or is everything predestined?

The story is told of a man who died and went to heaven and saw two lines, one line said "Predestined" and the other line said "Free Choice". Being a good Calvinist he got in the predestined line, and after working his way to the sign-in desk the angel asked him, "Why are you in this line?", at which the man replied, "Well, I saw the two lines and chose this one." The angel said, "Well you're in the wrong line, the free choice line is over there." So the man went over to the other line, and worked his way to the front, and at the desk the angel asked him, "Why are you in this line?", and the man said, "Somebody made me come here." And the angel said, "Well you're in the wrong line, this is the free will line, you need to go back to the other one."[20]

It gets so confusing, doesn't it? Predestination or free will? The debate's been going on for 2,000 years.

But Scripture is clear in many places that, even though God wills or wants certain things to happen, they don't always happen. That's because there's something else at play here.

For example:

Ezekiel 22:30, 31:

> *"I searched for a man among them who would build up the wall and stand in the gap before Me for the land (as an intercessor), so that I would not destroy it; but I found no one. Thus I have poured out My indignation on them; I have consumed them with the fire of My wrath; their way I have brought upon their heads," declares the <u>Lord God</u>.*

Question: What was God's will?
Answer: NOT to destroy the land.
Question: Did God's will come to pass?
Answer: No!

Question: And what or who was the determining factor?
Answer: A human being, or more precisely, the lack of a human being, standing in the gap as an intercessor.

"Is God always in control?" In fact, He is not always in control, sometimes mankind determines the outcome. This could be shown over and over in scripture.

You'll notice in the scripture verse that I've underlined the last words of verse 32, "declares the <u>Lord GOD</u>."

The New International Version reads, "declares the <u>Sovereign LORD</u>." But the Hebrew (the Old Testament was written primarily in Hebrew) doesn't use the word "Sovereign" here.

Actually, in the King James Version, the word "sovereign" is never used. It's translated that way in some modern translations like the New International Version or New Living Translation, but the real Hebrew word used here is, "Adonay (ad-ō-noý)," and means, "Lord, Master, Owner".

When we use the word "sovereign" in God-talk, it creates connotations that aren't necessarily true, so we have to be very careful. "But Tom, doesn't the Bible teach that God is "sovereign" even as we think of the word?" My answer would be, "Yes and no, it depends on how one defines the word *sovereign*."

There are a number of different nuances or aspects of the definition for the word "sovereign", let me give you three:

Sovereign
- Supreme in authority
- Supreme in rank or power
- Unrestricted

Some people will impose their Calvinistic theology by adding another nuance to the definition, "controls everything." But that's not actually in the definition. That's an addition. It would be more accurate to say, "God CAN control everything," because sometimes God chooses not to, He chooses to limit His direct control.

So, is God supreme in authority? Absolutely. Is God supreme in rank or power? Absolutely. Is God unrestricted? The answer to that is, "yes", but there is a caveat here. "Yes", because God is inherently unrestricted, but "no", because <u>He has chosen to restrict Himself in certain circumstances</u>!

Does God control everything? No! Does He have the authority and right to control everything? Yes! One might say God controls everything because He created a law called "sowing and reaping," and so when mankind reaps a negative consequence because they've sown a negative action, God is indirectly in control. He's the one who created that law.

But does God control and cause everything directly? No. To believe that means He caused Adam and Eve to sin. That's ridiculous.

If one believes that God controls everything, then they'd have to believe that it was God's will that the U.S. Supreme Court voted the way they did in Roe vs. Wade in 1973, subsequently causing 60 million babies to be murdered. Preposterous!

If one believes that God controls everything, then they'd have to believe that it was God's will for a man to rape a five-year-old girl. What kind of foolishness is that? It doesn't line up with common sense, scripture, or God's character of love.

I heard a nationally known pastor say regarding God, "He is governing history in every minute detail, there's not one molecule in the universe that is out of line with His purposes."[21] Of course, this is the classic Calvinist position. But if true, that means that when the molecules of King David's sperm fertilized the molecules of Bathsheba's egg, those molecules were perfectly in line with God's purpose, even though it was the act of adultery and contrary to God's commandment. So, David disobeyed God and obeyed God by the same act. I have a problem with that kind of thinking, even if it comes from the lips of a well-known pastor and teacher.

God is still omnipotent (all powerful), yet Ezekiel 22 shows us that God chose to restrict Himself to an intercessor's prayers and to the obedience of people!

John Wesley (1703-1791), with his brother Charles, founders of Methodist churches and Wesleyanism, said:

> *"God does nothing except in answer to prayer."*[22]

"God restricts Himself to us praying? And if we don't pray, it doesn't happen? Preposterous!" But is it? One time Jesus looked over the multitudes and saw the great need because they were distressed and He felt great compassion for them.

Question: What would be the obvious solution?
Answer: Jesus, just meet their needs!

But that's not what Jesus did. He said to do something else.

Matthew 9:37,38:

> Then He said to His disciples, *"The harvest is plentiful, but the workers are few. Therefore, **beseech the Lord of the harvest to send out workers** into His harvest."*

Jesus' response...pray! The New International Version reads, "ask the Lord of the harvest," and the New Living Translation says, "pray to the Lord who is in charge of the harvest."

Wait! God is the "Lord of the harvest", so why doesn't He just send workers into the harvest to minister to the people? Answer: He's waiting for us to pray, asking Him to do so!

Clearly, God has chosen to restrict Himself to our prayers in many cases. In Ezekiel 22, God's will did not come to pass! Therefore, "sovereign" does NOT mean that everything that happens on earth or in your life is God's will or from His hand!

God has generally chosen to limit Himself to responding to our prayers!

The problem is our traditional, religious thinking. And our religious traditional thinking is so ingrained in us that we naturally believe that everything that happens is God's will. "He's got the whole world in His hands!"

There are traditions of practice but there are also traditions of belief and thinking. In either case, these can keep us from fully understanding God's Word.

Mark 7:13:

> *... invalidating the word of God by your tradition which you have handed down; and you do many things such as that.*

We can negate the Word of God by erroneous thinking.

Here's an example of a portion of God's Word that Christians mess up because of religious, traditional, and erroneous thinking, and caution, I'm about to mess with your theology here.

Acts 5:33-37:

> *But when they heard this, they were cut to the quick and intended to kill them. But a Pharisee named Gamaliel, a teacher of the Law, respected by all the people, stood up in the Council and gave orders to put the men outside for a short time. And he said to them, "Men of Israel, take care what you propose to do with these men. For some time ago Theudas rose up, claiming to be somebody, and a group of about four hundred men joined up with him. But he was killed, and all who followed him were dispersed and came to nothing. After this man, Judas of Galilee rose up in the days of the census and drew away some people after him; he too perished, and all those who followed him were scattered.*

The next two verses (Vss 38-39) are what mess people up:

Acts 5:38-39

> *So in the present case, I say to you, stay away from these men and let them alone, for **if this plan or action is of men, it will be overthrown**; but **if it is of God, you will not be able to***

overthrow them; or else you may even be found fighting against God."

We generally quote these verses as if what Gamaliel said was true. But it's not true. "Well, if it's of man, it will fail, and if it's of God, it will certainly succeed." How many times have you heard that? How many times have you said that! But these were words spoken by an unsaved, unregenerate man!

Now thank God that He used it to get the Apostles out of jail. We are grateful, probably not as grateful as the Apostles. But, theologically, what Gamaliel said was not true.

If it's of man, it will fail? Really? Do you remember the people building the Tower of Babel in Genesis 11? They were all of one language and one purpose to build a tower up to heaven, and it says they were trying to do this to make a name for themselves, presumably to reach God and most likely then to dictate to God how they wanted things done on this earth.

But God saw their man-centered plan and dispersed the crowd by making them speak different languages so that they wouldn't understand each other, and so the building project stopped immediately. But here's what God said about their plan, and keep in mind, this was God Himself appraising the situation: Genesis 11:5-6

*The Lord came down to see the city and the tower which the sons of men had built. The Lord said, "Behold, they are one people, and they all have the same language. And this is what they began to do, and now **nothing which they purpose to do will be impossible for them**.*

Wait ... "nothing which they purpose to do will be impossible for them"! That's not THEIR OWN testimony of what they could achieve. That's GOD'S testimony of them! Now that flies in the face of what Gamaliel said, "If this plan is of men, it will be overthrown!"

The second part of Gamaliel's statements was, "If it's of God, you won't be able to stop it." Is that true? The answer is: yes and no. On a macro scale, regarding end-time events and the ultimate purposes of God for the world, yes; but on a micro scale, regarding your own life, church, ministry, or sometimes even a nation, no, it's not true. As I demonstrated from Ezekiel 22, God's will does not automatically come to pass.

We could make a list of churches and ministries that have failed because man got in the way and messed it up. Many would disagree with me here, but I believe the original vision of PTL and Heritage USA, with Jim and Tammy Bakker, was of God. But man got in the way and messed it up, and it failed.

Look at all the churches that have closed and become restaurants or banquet halls. These were churches that started with a vision from God. But those churches failed, many times because man got in the way and didn't change how they did things, continuing to do church like it was 1960; or they drifted away from a true gospel, or they became ingrown.

"If it's of God it will succeed?" No, not necessarily. We're thankful that God used Gamaliel's words to get the Apostles off the hook, but strictly speaking, his words weren't true. And yet Christians continue to parrot Gamaliel, "Like the Bible says, if it's not of God it will fail, and if it's of God it will succeed." Nope, not true.

There are numerous cases in scripture where God's will did not come pass! Ezekiel 22:30, 31 is just one.

In 1 Samuel 8, God wanted to set Himself up as Israel's King, but they looked around and saw all the other nations with kings, and so they wanted an earthly king as well. God didn't want to do it, but eventually gave in to their desire for a human king, but warning them that they made the wrong decision and it would cause them grief.

1 Samuel 8:5-7

> *"Now appoint a king for us to judge us like all the nations." But the thing was displeasing in the sight of Samuel when they said, "Give us a king to judge us." And Samuel prayed to the Lord. The Lord said to Samuel, "Listen to the voice of the people in regard to all that they say to you, for they have not rejected you, but they have rejected Me from being king over them.*

Question: What was God's will in the matter? Answer: For Israel NOT to have an earthly king. Question: Did God's will come to pass? Answer: No. Question: Who was the determining factor on whether God's will came to pass or not? Answer: Man.

On the flip side of the coin, there are some devil-inspired enterprises that are flourishing; pornography and false religions being examples. The fastest growing religion in the world is Islam—does this mean it's from God? No!

He's got the whole world in His hands? Everything that happens is from God? No! Many times we become the determining factor by whether we pray or yield to His control or not. It's not all God, because He gives us choices.

Deuteronomy 30:15-16,19-20

> *See, I have set before you today life and prosperity, and death and adversity; in that I command you today to love the LORD your God, to walk in His ways and to keep His commandments and His statutes and His judgments, that you may live and multiply, and that the LORD your God may bless you in the land where you are entering to possess it. ... I call heaven and earth to witness against you today, that I have set before you life and death, the blessing and the curse. So **choose life** in order that you may live, you and your descendants, by loving the LORD your God, by obeying His voice, and by holding fast to Him; for this is your life and the length of your days, that you may live in the land which the LORD swore to your fathers, to Abraham, Isaac, and Jacob, to give them.*

God gave mankind a multiple-choice test: life/blessing/prosperity or death/curse/adversity; and then said, "Choose." And just to make sure they didn't get all confused on this multiple-choice test, He gave them the correct answer ... "Choose life, blessing, and prosperity!"

Man's decisions have a part to play in whether God's will comes to pass or not. We see this in the ministry of Jesus, when He came to His hometown of Nazareth. As in every other place Jesus visited, His will was to heal and set people free. Did this happen? Were people healed in Nazareth?

Matthew 13:54,57-58

> *He came to His hometown and began teaching them in their synagogue, ... And they took offense at Him. But Jesus said to them, "A prophet is not without honor except in his hometown and in his own household." And He **did not** (Mark 6:5 says "**could not**") do many miracles there because of their unbelief.*

Was it His will to do miracles of healing? Yes. Did that happen? No. Why? Because of the people's hard hearts and unbelief. So who was the determining factor here, Jesus or the people? Answer: the people.

Is God always in control? No. Does He have the whole world in His hands? On a macro scale regarding the nations and eschatology (His plan for end-time events), yes. Yet, much of this world is influenced by man or Satan. It's interesting that scripture gives the devil some interesting titles, titles that reflect strong supernatural influence on this earth.

2 Corinthians 4:3-4

*And even if our gospel is veiled, it is veiled to those who are perishing, in whose case **the god of this world** has blinded the minds of the unbelieving so that they might not see the light of the gospel of the glory of Christ, who is the image of God.*

John 14:30

*I will not speak much more with you, for **the ruler of the world** is coming, and he has nothing in Me.*

John 12:31

*Now judgment is upon this world; now **the ruler of this world** will be cast out.*

Ephesians 2:2

*In which you formerly walked according to the course of this world, according to **the prince of the power of the air**, of the spirit that is now working in the sons of disobedience.*

Scripture is clear that the devil has real power here on earth. When Jesus was tempted in the wilderness by the devil, notice was Satan said:

Luke 4:6-7

*And the devil said to Him, "I will give You all this domain and its glory; **for it has been handed over to me**, and I give it to whomever I wish.*

What's interesting is, Jesus did not challenge Satan on his statement, for Jesus knew that it was true. The devil does have a measured, limited degree of authority and power.

1 John 5:19

We know that we are of God, and that the whole world lies in the power of the evil one.

And this statement was made AFTER the resurrection of Jesus Christ! "The whole world lies in the power of the evil one." But we sing, "He's got the whole world, in His hands." Not according to 1 John 5:19.

But what about other verses, like 1 Chronicles 29:11,12?

1 Chronicles 29:11-12

*Yours, O Lord, is the greatness and the power and the glory and the victory and the majesty, indeed **everything that is in the heavens and the earth; Yours is the dominion**, O Lord, and You exalt Yourself as head over all. Both riches and honor come from You, and **You rule over all**, and **in Your hand is power and might**; and it lies in Your hand to make great and to strengthen everyone.*

Does this contradict what Jesus said in 1 John 5:19? These words from 1 Chronicles 29 were made by David after seeing the size of the offering of money, gold and silver given by all of Israel's leaders for the building of the temple.

Everything that is in the heavens and the earth (is Yours) - Yours is the dominion – You rule over all – in Your hand is power and might.

We have two possibilities of interpretation for these statements. Did David mean:

1) Every little thing that happens on Planet Earth was caused by God and in line with His will?

or ...

2) Everything in heaven and earth belongs to God, ultimate authority belongs to God, He is all powerful, and He will rule and execute His plan for His people?

If you believe #1, to be consistent, you would have to believe that God caused David to commit adultery with Bathsheba and to murder her husband! You would have to believe that the tsunami that killed 250,000 people December 26, 2004 was God's will! You would have to believe the 6 million Jews wiped out by Hitler during World War II was God's will.

No, God is not always in control. God is not the only influence here on earth. Besides Him, there is fleshly, natural influence (mankind) and supernatural influence (Satan). Let us not fool ourselves into thinking that God is always in control, that He's got the whole world in His hands.

I believe the biblical principle is this:

*God is in control **to the degree** that we pray and yield to His control.*

Though this doesn't apply to macro issues like end-time events and God's overall plan of the ages, I do believe it's true for the more micro issues of our personal lives. God is a Gentleman and will not override our wills. He moves in our lives as we pray, surrender and yield to His influence and will. That is the essence of Romans 12:1.

Romans 12:1- 2

Therefore I urge you, brethren, by the mercies of God, to present your bodies a living and holy sacrifice, acceptable to God, which is your spiritual service of worship. And do not be conformed to this world, but be transformed by the renewing of your mind, so that you may prove what the will of God is, that which is good and acceptable and perfect.

As we align our thinking with His thinking by getting our minds renewed to God's Word, and as we present our lives in obedience to Him by surrendering to His Lordship, we experience living in His perfect will.

But what if we don't get our minds renewed or present our bodies to Him as instruments of obedience, can we still expect to experience God's *good, acceptable and perfect* will? If words mean anything, no, not according to this passage.

Next, in Part 2, we'll cover some teachings that are generally embraced by most Christians that are just plain erroneous. Christians can be hurt by their lack of knowledge.

Hosea 4:6

My people are destroyed for lack of knowledge.

Part 2

A Contrarian View of Christian Teaching

CHAPTER 5

To Teach You Something

Typically, answers are given about why bad things happen to good people that don't quite square with scripture, although they sound religious and right.

Before delving into the first of the most common answers to suffering that Christians many times give, let me cover two initial introductory points. The first has to do with this word "good" (why do *good* people suffer) and the second deals with suffering as part of God's will.

First, when looking at this question, "Why do bad things happen to good people", we must declare, as Jesus did in the Gospels, that no one is "good" but God alone.

Mark 10:17-18

> *As He was setting out on a journey, a man ran up to Him and knelt before Him, and asked Him, "Good Teacher, what shall I do to inherit eternal life?" And Jesus said to him, "Why do you call Me good?* **No one is good except God alone**.

One could even say there are no good people, so...argument over. The truth is, none of us are good!

Romans 3:10-12

> *There is none righteous, not even one; there is none who understands, there is none who seeks for God; all have turned aside, together they have become useless; there is none who does good, there is not even one."*

We all are sinners, none of us are good. Actually, the better question is, knowing that we are all sinners and fall woefully short of the glory of God (Romans 3:23), why do good things happen to any of us at all? We don't deserve any of it!

Lamentations 3:39

> *Why should any living mortal, or any man, offer complaint in view of his sins?*

Having said that, we do understand the question because we all know people who, although they sin and are not perfect, are still known to be very nice and caring people. OK, let's go with that. Why do bad things happen to basically good, nice, caring people? Chapters 11-20 cover that.

Secondly, many times Christians will say that suffering is the will of God, as seen in scripture. For example:

1 Peter 4:19

> *Therefore, those also who **suffer according to the will of God** shall entrust their souls to a faithful Creator in doing what is right.*

That phrase, "suffer according to the will of God" proves that there is a type of suffering that is in line with God's will. And even in verse 13 of the same chapter it talks about sharing in "the sufferings of Christ."

The problem is that Christians will use these two verses to say that ALL suffering is according to the will of God, and that is patently false.

In the context of the passage here in 1 Peter 4, what type of suffering is "according to the will of God"? We must keep verse 19 in context with what's being said in the previous verses.

1 Peter 4:12-19

> *Beloved, do not be surprised at the fiery ordeal among you, which comes upon you for your testing, as though some strange thing were happening to you; but to the degree that you share the sufferings of Christ, keep on rejoicing, so that also at the revelation of His glory you may rejoice with exultation. If you are **reviled for the name of Christ**, you are blessed, because the Spirit of glory and of God rests on you. Make sure that none*

*of you suffers as a murderer, or thief, or evildoer, or a troublesome meddler; but **if anyone suffers as a Christian**, he is not to be ashamed, but is to glorify God in this name. For it is time for judgment to begin with the household of God; and if it begins with us first, what will be the outcome for those who do not obey the gospel of God? And if it is with difficulty that the righteous is saved, what will become of the godless man and the sinner? Therefore, those also who suffer according to the will of God shall entrust their souls to a faithful Creator in doing what is right.*

Notice "reviled for the name of Christ" and "if anyone suffers as a Christian," in other words, for being a Christian. The clear context of the suffering mentioned in this passage is persecution, not disease, accidents or calamity.

Healing, protection and provision are blessings afforded us in Jesus Christ. I believe them to be blessings promised to us in God's Word. We have been redeemed from sickness.

Psalm 103:2,3

Bless the Lord, O my soul, and forget none of His benefits; who pardons all your iniquities, who heals all your diseases.

We are promised protection.

Psalm 91:10-12

No evil will befall you, nor will any plague come near your tent. For He will give His angels charge concerning you, to guard you in all your ways. They will bear you up in their hands, that you do not strike your foot against a stone.

We are promised material provision.

Philippians 4:19

And my God will supply all your needs according to His riches in glory in Christ Jesus.

What we are NOT promised is to be free from persecution.

John 15:20

> *Remember the word that I said to you, 'A slave is not greater than his master.' If they persecuted Me, they will also persecute you;*

2 Timothy 3:12

> *Indeed, all who desire to live godly in Christ Jesus will be persecuted.*

Persecution for being a Christian is the only suffering we have not been redeemed from, and therefore it is the only suffering that is "according to the will of God." And when 1 Peter 4:13 says "sharing in the sufferings of Christ", it is talking about exactly that, the reviling and maltreatment that Christ experienced on Good Friday.

We need to stop using "suffering according to the will of God" to foist upon people this erroneous idea that sickness, accidents, and calamity are God's will, because to do so is to take these verses of out context.

To Teach You Something

Having touched on these two introductory points, let me now cover the crux of this chapter. If you've been a Christian for any length of time, you have heard teaching that, although sounding right, does not square with scripture.

Here in Part 2, let me cover the predominant answers Christians give for suffering that do not align with a serious study of God's Word, starting with number one; *to teach you something.*

We've all heard this one. "God has allowed this to happen because He is using it to teach you something." Here again, we have God as the causal agent. What's clearly implied by the statement is that He allowed it because He caused it, and He caused it in order to teach you a lesson of some kind.

But let's examine this in the light of scripture and find out HOW God teaches His children.

Let me start by asking you a question—how do YOU teach your children? Do you teach your children by intentionally harming them?

Does a parent teach his child not to touch a hot stove by placing the child's hand on a hot stove? No! There are civil laws against such horrible behavior! If we would never do such a thing, then be sure, our Heavenly Father, who is a far better and loving parent than any of us, would never do such a thing either.

Matthew 7:11

If you then, being evil, know how to give good gifts to your children, how much more will your Father who is in heaven give what is good to those who ask Him!

We're evil compared to our Heavenly Father, and we would only give and do nice things to our children. Certainly God, a far more loving and kind parent, would only do and give good things as well.

I don't believe God brings into our lives, in order to teach us, anything that He has already redeemed us from as a result of the work of the cross (redemption from sickness, disease, pain, poverty, tragedy).

James 1:13 (Weymouth New Testament)

Let no one say when passing through trial, "My temptation is from God;" for God is incapable of being tempted to do evil, and He Himself tempts no one.

It says NOT to say that, yet a lot of people continue to say it, "God's putting you through this trial!"

James 1:17

Every good thing given and every perfect gift is from above, coming down from the Father of lights

God will not bring into a believer's life, in order to teach them, the effects of the curse that came into this world as a result of sin, things mentioned in Deuteronomy 28:15ff. The things mentioned in that passage (sickness, disease, poverty, mental oppression) are all a result of the curse of the law. But...we have been redeemed from those things!

Galatians 3:13

Christ redeemed us from the curse of the Law, having become a curse for us—for it is written, "Cursed is everyone who hangs on a tree."

Now, does God chastise and correct His children? Of course He does, He's our Father, but how? Hebrews 12 talks about this.

Hebrews 12:5,6

*You have **forgotten the exhortation** which is addressed to you as sons, "My son, do not regard lightly the discipline (KJV - chastening) of the Lord, nor faint when you are reproved by Him; for those whom the Lord loves He disciplines."*

In our minds, chastisement means "punishment," but that is not the meaning in the Greek language. Chastening or chastisement carries the idea of child training and education, not punishment. Does God chastise (correct, train) us by putting sickness and disease on us? No!

How does He correct us? It says you've "forgotten the exhortation which is addressed to you as sons."

It's an exhortation with words! He exhorts us with His Word! How do you teach and train your children? With words. The word "chastise" or "chastisement" in Greek carries the idea of child training. Earthly parents don't harm their children in order to train them, and neither does our Heavenly Father. He corrects us through His Word. Notice the purposes of God mentioned in 2 Timothy 3:16.

2 Timothy 3:16

*All Scripture is inspired by God and profitable for **teaching**, for **reproof**, for **correction**, for **training** in righteousness.*

God's way of training, reproof and correction is speaking to us through His Word. In fact, correction through God's Word can actually hurt more than a whipping! I've experienced it many times!

Proverbs 17:10

A rebuke goes deeper into one who has understanding than a hundred blows into a fool.

God doesn't send evil into our lives to correct us so that we turn around and make a change.

Romans 2:4

> Or do you think lightly of the riches of His kindness and tolerance and patience, not knowing that **the kindness of God leads you to repentance?**

The KINDNESS of God leads us to repentance, not the suffering of horrible things.

There is another place in the New Testament where it says God reproves and disciplines us. That's in the book of Revelation. In Revelation 2 and 3, Jesus is addressing seven churches. In each case, Jesus tells them some things they're doing well, but He also corrects and chastises each church.

Revelation 3:19

> Those whom I love, I reprove and discipline; therefore, be zealous and repent.

Out of seven churches in Revelation 2 and 3, only two were not corrected by Jesus. And how did Jesus reprove and discipline these churches? He corrected them with His words!

Revelation 2:4-5 - Ephesus

> But I have this against you, that you have left your first love. Therefore remember from where you have fallen, and <u>repent</u> and do the deeds you did at first; or else I am coming to you and will remove your lampstand out of its place—unless you repent.

Revelation 2:14-15 – Pergamum

> But I have a few things against you, because you have there some who hold the teaching of Balaam, who kept teaching Balak to put a stumbling block before the sons of Israel, to eat things sacrificed to idols and to commit acts of immorality. So you also have some who in the same way hold the teaching of the Nicolaitans. Therefore <u>repent</u>.

Revelation 2:20-21 – Thyatira

But I have this against you, that you tolerate the woman Jezebel ... I gave her time to repent, and she does not want to repent of her immorality.

Revelation 3:1-3 – Sardis

He who has the seven Spirits of God and the seven stars, says this: 'I know your deeds, that you have a name that you are alive, but you are dead. Wake up, and strengthen the things that remain, which were about to die; for I have not found your deeds completed in the sight of My God. So remember what you have received and heard; and keep it, and <u>repent</u>.

Revelation 3:15-19 Laodicea

'I know your deeds, that you are neither cold nor hot; I wish that you were cold or hot. So because you are lukewarm, and neither hot nor cold, I will spit you out of My mouth. Because you say, "I am rich, and have become wealthy, and have need of nothing," and you do not know that you are wretched and miserable and poor and blind and naked, I advise you to buy from Me gold refined by fire so that you may become rich, and white garments so that you may clothe yourself, and that the shame of your nakedness will not be revealed; and eye salve to anoint your eyes so that you may see. Those whom I love, I reprove and discipline; therefore be zealous and <u>repent</u>.

Now to be clear, God HAS caused judgment to fall upon unrepented wicked behavior (e.g. – Noah's flood of Genesis 6,7; Ananias and Sapphira in Acts 5:1-11; Herod in Acts 12:23; the man continuing in sexual immorality without repentance in 1 Corinthians 5:5; Jezebel and her followers in Revelation 3:22-23), but I don't believe God causes evil to come upon His people who are endeavoring to walk before Him in love and truth. He does not use evil to teach or train His own dear children who are walking before Him in integrity.

About this time someone will pipe up and say, "Well, if sickness, disease, poverty or calamity caused the person to learn and become a better person, then in the end we can't classify it as *evil*." But that is just playing around with the English language. We all have an inherent and intuitive sense of what is good and evil, so let's not play games and confuse the two. Scripture warns us against messing up the clear definition of good and evil.

Isaiah 5:20

Woe to those who call evil good, and good evil

We all know intuitively that these things are evil. Let's not start calling evil things like sickness, disease, calamity and tragedy good.

That said, God IS smart enough to bring good things out of bad situations. He will take the opportunity to teach and train us if we suffer and experience bad things. If we train our child with words, "Don't touch the hot stove," and they go against that training and get burned, we naturally, as any good parent would, say, "I told you not to touch the hot stove, so from now on, learn from this and don't touch it." God will do the same, but He's not the one causing us to suffer.

Chapter 6

To Bring Good Out of It

There are six main responses to suffering which Christians give that I find don't add up with scripture. In the previous chapter, we covered the first one, the "in order to teach you something" response.

Another response for human suffering which Christians sometimes give is that God causes suffering so that He can turn it around and bring good out of it...kind of like a cat and mouse game; grab the mouse (bad) and then let it go (good).

This reminds me of firemen who start fires so that they can rush to the scene and put it out, thereby being proclaimed a hero.

The idea that God causes suffering so that He can turn it around and bring good out of it, comes from a misinterpretation of Romans 8:28. This verse is quoted more than any other by Christians when bad things happen.

Romans 8:28

And we know that God causes all things to work together for good to those who love God, to those who are called according to His purpose.

You can bet this will be repeated this once hearing that something bad happened to someone: "Well, like the Bible says, God causes all things to work together for the good." Take note, they don't quote the rest of that verse (*for those that love God and are called according to His purpose*).

So is this a blanket statement that says, in every case, God will cause something good to come out of something bad?

The truth is, there are a whole lot of people who have had bad things happen to them or their families who never recovered. In some cases, they even committed suicide. There are others who have become atheists or dropped out of church because of bad things that have happened to them or their loved ones. For many people, Romans 8:28 is an unfulfilled promise or worse—a downright lie.

First of all, let's set the record straight here, the verse doesn't say God causes all things, yet that's how some Christians interpret it. It says God causes all things to work out *for the good for those who love God and are called according to His purpose.* It's funny how Christians insert a meaning into a verse that just isn't there. But let's go deeper.

God causing all things to work out for the good is not automatic or unconditional! It has conditions and, according to the verse, can only be applied to:

1. The person who loves God, and
2. The person who is walking in God's purposes for their lives.

If someone is not a Christian and/or not actively loving God through His Son Jesus Christ; or, he or she is not flowing with God's purposes or will for their lives, then God's will won't necessarily result. If God is not even a factor in their lives, or if someone is shutting God out of their lives, then the promise of Romans 8:28 doesn't apply to them.

But, if someone loves God and is walking in His purposes for their life, yes, God will cause good to come out of bad as they continue to love and trust Him.

Closely connected to this idea that God automatically brings good out of bad, is another...that "everything happens for a reason." I've heard this more times than I can count. "Well, you know, everything happens for a reason." We'll touch on this in Chapter 10.

Joseph

Many times people will bring up the story of Joseph from the Old Testament to make the point that God causes suffering for a reason.

Joseph's brothers sold him as a slave to Egypt (Genesis 37). Eventually God turned the whole thing around and Joseph became second-in-command over all of Egypt. Because he was in this influential position directly under Pharoah, Joseph was able to, as revealed to him in a vision by God, store food for seven years before seven years of famine, thereby providing food for all the people, including his own family.

In the end, Joseph, as he responds to his groveling brothers, says this:

Genesis 50:19-20

"Do not be afraid, for am I in God's place? As for you, you meant evil against me, but God meant it for good in order to bring about this present result, to preserve many people alive."

Of course, God causing Joseph's suffering was Joseph's own natural deduction, seen from his perspective. It would have been anybody's deduction. But the real question here is...was God causing Joseph's suffering or was this a case of God bringing good out of bad?

People make the case that God caused Joseph's suffering to eventually provide for His people. But let's think about this.

If God caused Joseph's suffering, it means that God designed and created all the links in the chain of the story, therefore it means that:

1. God caused Joseph to shoot off his big mouth by prematurely revealing a vision that he had about his brothers serving him (Genesis 37:9-11).
2. God caused Joseph's brothers to plot to murder him (Genesis 37:18ff).
3. God caused Joseph's brother to sell him as a slave (Genesis 37:25ff, Acts 7:9).
4. God caused Joseph's brothers to lie to their father (Genesis 37:19,31ff).

In short, they say, it means God inspired and caused evil to be committed in order to produce a positive result. I don't buy it. God doesn't commit evil.

Habakkuk 1:13

Your eyes are too pure to approve evil, And You can not look on wickedness with favor.

And God doesn't tempt others to commit evil.

James 1:13

Let no one say when he is tempted, "I am being tempted by God"; for God cannot be tempted by evil, and He Himself does not tempt anyone.

Listen, God doesn't need to design, lead or inspire people to act wickedly so that He can produce a favorable end! God is an infinite God who has infinite ways of producing a good result. He could have ensured that Joseph was second in charge of all of Egypt through a myriad of ways. God doesn't inspire and cause people to commit evil so that He can turn it around.

Acts 7:9

The patriarchs became jealous of Joseph and sold him into Egypt. Yet God was with him.

God didn't cause the patriarchs (Joseph's brothers) to become jealous and sell him. God doesn't cause evil. But in the midst of evil and suffering, God was with Joseph and did an amazing turnaround.

Joseph's story is the story of God bringing good out of bad, which, by the way, God is a Master at doing. It's much like what the Apostle Paul said regarding his persecution.

Philippians 1:12-13

Now I want you to know, brethren, that my circumstances have turned out for the greater progress of the gospel, so that my imprisonment in the cause of Christ has become well known throughout the whole praetorian guard and to everyone else.

This is the essence of Romans 8:28.

Romans 8:28

And we know that God causes all things to work together for good to those who love God, to those who are called according to His purpose.

God doesn't design and cause bad things to happen, He is the One who turns it around for the good.

What's implied by people is that everything happens for a reason, and it's God who is causing it all to happen for some divine reason. I hope by now I've showed you that scripturally, this isn't true. If not, keep reading because the whole of this book challenges that idea.

The Blind Man of John 9

Sometimes people will bring up John 9, the story of the blind man that Jesus healed. The way the story reads sounds like God intentionally made sure the man was born blind in order to eventually heal him, so that God could get glory from the miracle (as if there was a shortage of blind people around at the time without having to do that). Let's read the story.

John 9:1-7

> As He passed by, He saw a man blind from birth. And His disciples asked Him, "Rabbi, who sinned, this man or his parents, that he would be born blind?" Jesus answered, "It was neither that this man sinned, nor his parents; but it was so that the works of God might be displayed in him. We must work the works of Him who sent Me as long as it is day; night is coming when no one can work. While I am in the world, I am the Light of the world." When He had said this, He spat on the ground, and made clay of the spittle, and applied the clay to his eyes, and said to him, "Go, wash in the pool of Siloam" (which is translated, Sent). So he went away and washed, and came back seeing.

"See! It says right there that he was born blind so that God's work of healing could be displayed in him!"

Just up front, does that sound like a God of love? 1 John 4:16 says, "God is love." Even before explaining this, does the idea that God intentionally ensures someone is born blind so that they can eventually be healed, sound logical? Does it sound like a God of love would do that...to have someone born blind just so that sometime in the future, say when the guy was forty-five years old, He could heal him?

The problem is in the punctuation. We have to remember that there is no punctuation in the Greek language; no periods, commas, or capital letters. In Greek, words just run together, and translators insert punctuation where they think it should go. But punctuation isn't inspired by God, the words are.

One can totally change the meaning of a sentence or paragraph just by slightly changing the punctuation.

Let's eat, mommy.
Let's eat mommy!

We're going to learn to cut and paste, kids.
We're going to learn to cut and paste kids!

In Scripture, the same thing can happen. Here is John 9:1-5 from Young's Literal Translation (what the Greek is literally saying, word-for-word). I'm only adjusting (respelling) one word, from "behoveth" to "behooves" because "eth" words sound weird today. Here's what it literally says after adjusting just the punctuation:

Jesus answered, `Neither did this one sin nor his parents, but that the works of God may be manifested in him; it behooves me to be working the works of Him who sent me while it is day; night doth come, when no one is able to work: -- when I am in the world, I am a light of the world.'

The way that passage is punctuated implies the man was born blind so that God could heal him. But, let's take the exact same passage, word-for-word, and make some slight changes to the punctuation:

Jesus answered, `Neither did this one sin nor his parents.' But, that the works of God may be manifested in him, it behooves me to be working the works of Him who sent me while it is day. Night doth come when no one is able to work. When I am in the world, I am a light of the world.'

The exact same words from the Greek, but with a completely different meaning. Let's take the passage directly from the King James Version. Here is how the passage, with its current punctuation, reads:

> *Jesus answered, Neither hath this man sinned, nor his parents: but that the works of God should be made manifest in him. I must work the works of him that sent me, while it is day: the night cometh, when no man can work. As long as I am in the world, I am the light of the world.*

Now let's see the same passage, same words, only changing punctuation:

> *Jesus answered, Neither hath this man sinned, nor his parents. But, that the works of God should be made manifest in him, I must work the works of him that sent me while it is day. The night cometh when no man can work. As long as I am in the world, I am the light of the world.*

There's a significant change of meaning there. In one instance it sounds like God made the man blind in order to heal him. In the other instance it doesn't sound like that at all, but rather that Jesus was there to manifest the works of God for the man by healing him.

The question asked by the disciples was, "Who sinned that this man was born blind like this, the man or his parents?" Jesus answered in one succinct sentence, "Neither did this one sin nor his parents." Period.

Then Jesus goes on to say that it's time that He gets busy and do the works of the Father because there will come a time when He's not there. Now I'm giving a pretty close paraphrase to Young's Literal:

> *Jesus answered, 'Neither did this one sin nor his parents.' But, so that the works of God may be manifested in him, it behooves Me to get busy and do the works of the Father while I'm here and available. The time is coming when it will be dark, when I am taken out of the world and not here to heal the man. When I am in the world, I'm the light that can manifest God's works." And then Jesus proceeded to heal the man.*

Jesus was saying, "But, that the works of God may be manifested in him, I need to get busy and heal him!"

In addition to this, we have the Greek word *hina*, usually translated "that" or "so that", followed by a verb in the subjective mood. "So that the works of God may be manifested in him." When this is the case, there are two possibilities of meaning, either expressing purpose or command, and there's a significant difference.[23] Context along with harmonizing with the rest of Scripture dictates which one should be used. Here's the difference in how they would read.

Purpose: "[He was born blind] so that God's works might be revealed in him." NRSV
Command: "[He was born blind], but let the works of God be revealed in him."

Quite a difference. Greg Boyd, in his book, *God at War*, talks about this verse:

> *The verse should not be interpreted as suggesting that God's will is behind this man's blindness. ... The original verse does not say that "he was born blind so that God's works might be revealed." The Greek simply has hina with the aorist subjunctive passive of phaneroo ("to manifest") and can readily be translated as, "But let the works of God be manifested."*[24]

That's what I believe to be the correct interpretation to this passage. I don't believe for one minute that God intentionally created the man blind so that he could suffer almost his entire life, so that on that particular day Jesus could heal him. There were plenty of blind people around, so that idea just doesn't make sense, nor does is harmonize with the rest of scripture. God doesn't make people suffer just so He can bring something good out of it.

Chapter 7

To Test Your Faith

In the previous two chapters we covered two common responses to suffering that Christians give:

1) God causes suffering to teach you something.
2) God causes suffering to bring good out of it.

Another common response to suffering by Christians is to say, "Well, God is testing you, He's bringing this adversity into your life to test your faith."

Again, God is claimed to be the causal agent here, and He's bringing storms and adversity into your life just to see if you'll pass the test. Evidently God is not omniscient and doesn't know the future, so He anxiously waits to see what you're going to do (open theism), hoping that you'll pass the test.

They also say that the reason God is testing you is to develop your faith. Let's address this by making two points.

1. God doesn't test or tempt with evil.

I maintain that sin, death, sickness, disease (which is incipient death), physical and mental disabilities, calamity, premature death due to tragedy or disease, poverty, mental illness and oppression—are all a result of the fall of man in Genesis 3, and fundamentally are NOT God's will for His people. All those things came in at the fall and will disappear when we're in heaven.

Additionally, this is not what we see in the life of Jesus Christ. When Jesus was here on the earth, He healed and set people free from all those things. Why? Because they weren't from Him, they were of the devil.

Acts 10:38

You know of Jesus of Nazareth, how God anointed Him with the Holy Spirit and with power, and how He went about doing good

> *and healing all who were **oppressed by the devil**, for God was with Him.*

Luke 13:16

> *And this woman, a daughter of Abraham as she is, **whom Satan has bound for eighteen long years**, should she not have been released from this bond on the Sabbath day?"*

Jesus didn't put those things on people. He released them from those types of things! His mission was to undo what Satan had done.

1 John 3:8

> *The Son of God appeared for this purpose, to destroy the works of the devil.*

God is NOT going to employ the works of the devil to discipline His children. As stated in Chapter 5, the problem happens when we confuse good with evil.

Isaiah 5:20

> *Woe to those who call evil good, and good evil; who substitute darkness for light and light for darkness; who substitute bitter for sweet and sweet for bitter!*

If we had a ledger, good things would be on one side and evil things on the another. Good comes from God and evil comes from the devil. Evil things are a result of man's sinful fall in the Garden of Eden.

I believe this is Theology 101...God good, devil bad. Good things come from God.

James 1:17

> *Every good gift and every perfect gift is from above, and comes down from the Father of lights, with whom there is no variation or shadow of turning.*

Bad things come from the enemy.

John 10:10

The thief comes only to steal and kill and destroy; I came that they may have life, and have it abundantly.

If there is stealing, killing and destroying going on, it's from Satan. Good comes from God, evil comes from the enemy.

Good	Evil
Health	Sickness & disease & pain
Long life	Premature death
Protection, safety	Accidents/Calamity/Tragedy
A sound mind	Mental illness & oppression
Purpose & meaning	Feeling of insignificance
Wisdom & guidance	Confusion & wandering
Provision	Poverty & lack
Faith, peace, joy	Fear, worry, terror
Love	Hate, envy, jealousy

If we were to look at Deuteronomy 28 (and we won't for space and time), the first fourteen verses are the blessings that come from walking with and obeying God. From verse fifteen on the chapter describes the curse of the law, and it is a pretty comprehensive list. But because of the cross, we have been redeemed from the things named as curses.

Galatians 3:13

Christ redeemed us from the curse of the Law, having become a curse for us—for it is written, "Cursed is everyone who hangs on a tree."

Here's my point...God is NOT going to bring into a Christian's life, in order to test him, things on the right side of the ledger, things that are fundamentally evil! How can I say this?

James 1:13

Let no one say when he is tempted, "I am being tempted by God"; for God cannot be tempted by evil, and He Himself does not tempt anyone.

God is NOT going to test or tempt people using evil. Period. He brings good to His children, not evil and disaster.

Jeremiah 29:11

"For I know the plans I have for you," declares the LORD, "plans to prosper you and not to harm you, plans to give you hope and a future. (NIV)

He's not going to bring the suffering of terrible adversity (right side of ledger) in order to test people. That just doesn't reconcile with scripture. And yet Christians say this all the time when people experience suffering.

To be clear, I'm not saying God doesn't test, but that He doesn't test <u>with evil</u>. He'll test with good however. He'll test with good? How? Let me explain.

You'll hear a whole teaching series on giving and tithing and then, what happens? You get a significant raise, promotion or financial windfall. Are you going to tithe? God's testing you. That's a good test, one we all look forward to.

You'll read in scripture or a book, or hear a sermon on spiritual gifts and volunteering, and God is testing you to see if you'll get off the bench as a spectator and get in the game.

You'll read or hear a sermon on sharing Christ with others, and then you're put in a position at the water cooler at work where someone brings up religion, God or heaven. What are you going to do, share or keep quiet?

You'll hear a sermon series on community and being knit together in love as members of the Body of Christ, and then a new session of small groups begins. What are you going to do...connect in community or remain isolated? God is testing you.

God does test, but He doesn't test with evil and suffering. We all need to correct our thinking on this so that it lines up with the Word of God. Let no man say when he's being tested or tempted with evil, that it's coming from God! And yet, that's exactly what Christians say all the time!

So point 1, God doesn't tempt or test with evil.

2. Trials of adversity develop patience, not faith!

Another thing people say is that God's testing you in order to develop your faith. They get this idea from James 1, but the passage doesn't say that at all.

James 1:2-4

*Consider it all joy, my brethren, when you encounter various trials, knowing that **the testing of your faith produces endurance**. And let endurance have its perfect result, so that you may be perfect and complete, lacking in nothing.*

It doesn't say that trials, storms or adversity produces faith, it says they produce patience! And the truth is—you had better have your faith developed BEFORE the storm comes!

Luke 6:47-49

*Everyone who comes to Me and hears My words and acts on them, I will show you whom he is like: he is like a man building a house, who dug deep and **laid a foundation on the rock**; and when a flood occurred, the torrent burst against that house and could not shake it, because it had been well built. But the one who has heard and has not acted accordingly, is like a man who built a house on the ground without any foundation; and the torrent burst against it and immediately it collapsed, and the ruin of that house was great."*

The time to have that foundation laid, a developed faith in God, is BEFORE the storm comes. And where does faith come from? From tests and trials? No, from God's Word.

Romans 10:17

So then faith comes by hearing, and hearing by the word of God. (NKJV)

Faith comes from reading, studying, meditating and engaging with God's Word. Faith does not come from suffering and trials. If that were the case, most suffering people would be full of faith, but that's not true.

What IS developed in tests and trials is patience and endurance. From James 1, "knowing that the testing of your faith produces endurance." Endurance is the thing that is worked and developed in trials and adversity. As we go through a trial and adversity, we put to work and develop the force of endurance, much the same as a runner develops endurance through time put in running.

It's time we stop saying, "You're suffering because God is testing your faith."

God did test Abraham (Genesis 22), but that wasn't because He didn't know what Abraham would do. I believe God tested Abraham in order to give a prophetic foretelling of the sacrificing of His own Son, Jesus Christ, on the cross. Additionally, the test didn't produce or develop Abraham's faith. Abraham's faith was developed BEFORE the test. The test manifested an already-developed faith.

God Won't Give You More Than You Can Handle

Closely related to this "God is testing you" response, is another, that "God won't give you more than you can handle." How many times have we all heard that? This is a skewed interpretation from 1 Corinthians 10.

1 Corinthians 10:13

> *No temptation has overtaken you but such as is common to man; and God is faithful, **who will not allow you to be tempted beyond what you are able**, but with the temptation will provide the way of escape also, so that you will be able to endure it.*

Some Christians take what is said here and turn it into, "God won't give you more than you can handle," meaning, suffering adversity. But the verse doesn't say that. So let's go to scripture and find out what it really says.

The key is understanding the verse is to understand the context of the passage. The verses before verse 13 are talking about the temptation to sin, NOT suffering adversity.

1 Corinthians 10:6-8

Now these things happened as examples for us, so that we would not crave evil things as they also craved. Do not be idolaters, as some of them were; as it is written, "The people sat down to eat and drink, and stood up to play." Nor let us act immorally, as some of them did.

Temptation to sin is the subject, and Paul didn't want the Corinthians to be lifted up in pride or be arrogant enough to think they couldn't be tempted as well. He says in the next verse:

1 Corinthians 10:12

Therefore let him who thinks he stands take heed that he does not fall.

Immediately following this is verse 13, our main verse:

No temptation has overtaken you but such as is common to man; and God is faithful, who will not allow you to be tempted beyond what you are able, but with the temptation will provide the way of escape also, so that you will be able to endure it.

The context and subject here is being tempted to sin. It is NOT talking about suffering adversity, calamity or trials.

He will not allow the temptation to sin to be more than you can stand or endure. How will God do this? It says that when you are tempted to sin, He will show you a way out of that temptation! It is not talking about suffering adversity.

So the subject is a way out of temptation to sin. When people just give a blanket proclamation, "God won't give you more than you can handle," it's implied that God is the one doing it. This is NOT the meaning of 1 Corinthians 10:13, so we need to stop using it that way.

Sometimes we say things like this ("God won't give you more than you can handle") thinking that we're helping people. In reality, we're not.

I saw (on YouTube) Rabbi Harold S. Kushner (Author of *When Bad Things Happen to Good People*) talking about a lady he had met and talked to at a conference. The lady was Harriet Schiff, author of the book, *The Bereaved Parent*. Harriet lost her young son on the operating table when he underwent surgery for a congenital heart problem. A Rabbi came to the hospital, and said to her, "Harriet, I know this is a hard time for you, but you'll be alright because God never sends us more of a burden then we can bear." [25]

Harriet's very first thought was, "It's my fault that Robbie died. If I had been a weaker person, God would never have done this to me."

The very statement intended to comfort had the opposite effect. We need to be careful. The truth is, there are lots of people who have experienced things that they WEREN'T able to endure, it was more than what they could bear. Sometimes they even abandoned their faith in God. Sometimes they abandoned life itself.

CHAPTER 8

Paul's Thorn in the Flesh

To many people, the idea that God doesn't afflict people with suffering is new, perhaps even radical. If you've been a Christian for a good length of time, you've probably heard it preached that sometimes God has people suffer so He can bring good out of it and/or get glory from it. Normally it's at this point they bring up the Apostle Paul and his thorn in the flesh.

Because this idea is so prevalent, and because it takes some explaining to undo past erroneous teaching, I felt the topic of Paul's thorn in the flesh deserved its own chapter. Paul's thorn in the flesh is mentioned in 2 Corinthians 12.

2 Corinthians 12:7-9

*Because of the surpassing greatness of the revelations, for this reason, to keep me from exalting myself, there was given me a **thorn in the flesh, a messenger of Satan** to **torment** me—to keep me from exalting myself! Concerning this I implored the Lord three times that it might leave me. And He has said to me, "My grace is sufficient for you, for power is perfected in weakness." Most gladly, therefore, I will rather boast about my weaknesses, so that the power of Christ may dwell in me.*

Let's break this down.

Surpassing greatness of revelations

Regarding "revelations," Paul here is talking about something he said in the previous verses.

2 Corinthians 12:1-6

> *Boasting is necessary, though it is not profitable; but I will go on to **visions and revelations** of the Lord. I know a man in Christ who fourteen years ago—whether in the body I do not know, or out of the body I do not know, God knows—such a man was caught up to the third heaven. And I know how such a man—whether in the body or apart from the body I do not know, God knows—was caught up into Paradise and heard inexpressible words, which a man is not permitted to speak. On behalf of such a man I will boast; but **on my own behalf I will not boast**, except in regard to my weaknesses. **For if I do wish to boast I will not be foolish**, for I will be speaking the truth; but I refrain from this, so that no one will credit me with more than he sees in me or hears from me.*

Almost all scholars believe that Paul was talking about himself here.[26] Think about it, why would Paul boast about someone else and then be given a thorn in the flesh because of it? So this was an experience that happened to Paul. God did something special, like the Apostle John, He gave Paul a vision by taking him up to heaven or Paradise. The experience was so vivid and real that Paul couldn't tell if he was experiencing it in his body or out of his body. During this experience, he received glorious revelations from the Lord...revelation and truth so deep that he wasn't permitted to go into detail about them after the experience. Even though Paul would, in the natural, have a desire and right to boast about this incredible experience, Paul said, "on my own behalf I will not boast" and, "for if I wish to boast I will not be foolish."

2 Corinthians 12:6 NKJV

> **Lest anyone** *should think of me above what he sees me to be or hears from me.*

I venture to say that it wasn't Paul that was the problem, it was the possibility that others might exalt him because of his experience and revelations. As a result, Paul would travel far and wide with these revelations and do great damage to the kingdom of darkness. He had to be slowed down.

2 Corinthians 12:6

> *So that no one* will credit me with more than he sees in me or hears from me.

The problem wasn't with Paul, it was with others. For example, in Acts 14:11-13, after praying for a lame man and seeing him healed, the people rushed upon Paul and called him a god and were going to do sacrifices to him. Talk about powerful influence! Of course, Paul didn't permit that.

If I had an enemy or didn't like someone because they were getting too much attention from people and carrying too much influence, there's nothing I'd rather do to curtail their influence than by taking an action that would bust them down to size. If the devil saw that too many people were being drawn to Paul and his revelations of Jesus Christ and the message of grace, there's nothing more he'd like to do than do something to Paul to either stop or slow down the message.

There was given to me

Some people will see the words, *there was given to me,* and with their invisible religious pencil add, "by God." But it doesn't say that. In fact, it tells us right in the passage who the thorn in the flesh was from: *a messenger of Satan.* It couldn't be any clearer. Turn that invisible religious pencil around and use its eraser to scratch out those invisible words "by God", because those words aren't in there.

A thorn in the flesh

Someone once said that Paul's thorn has stuck more people than any other type. It is a thorn that causes people to believe that God is behind their sickness.

"Thorn in the flesh" is an idiomatic expression, much like saying "pain in the neck" (or other places). It's used five other times in scripture, and never does it mean sickness. The expression is always used for people who caused trouble. For example, in Numbers 33, God told the Israelites to drive out the inhabitants of the land, and then God warned them what would happen if they didn't.

Numbers 33:55

> *But if you do not drive out the inhabitants of the land from before you, then it shall come about that those whom you let remain of them will become as **pricks in your eyes** and as **thorns in your sides**, and they will trouble you in the land in which you live.*

The term meant people who would harass and torment them. We see the same thing in Joshua when he warned the people to obey God and not become like the other nations and the implications if they did.

Joshua 23:13

> *They will be a snare and a trap to you, and a **whip on your sides** and **thorns in your eyes**, until you perish from off this good land which the Lord your God has given you.*

Every time the term is used it means people who would torment you. (See also Judges 2:3, Ezekiel 28:44). Keeping this in mind, we must allow the passage to name exactly who or what this thorn was.

A Messenger of Satan

> *There was given me a thorn in the flesh, a **messenger of Satan** to torment me.*

The thorn in the flesh wasn't from God, but from Satan. The "messenger of Satan" referenced here is one of two possible things: either a person (for example, a legalistic Jew sent from Jerusalem to follow Paul around and stir up trouble for him), or an evil spirit (who would do the same thing).

The word "messenger" here in the Greek is "aggelos" (pronounced *angelos*), where we get our word "angel" from. For example, in Revelation 2 and 3, *aggelos* is translated *angel*.

Revelation 2:1

> *To the **angel** of the church in Ephesus write ...*

Same Greek word. *Aggelos* is translated "angel" all seven times in those two chapters of Revelation. In the New Testament this Greek word is translated 7 times as "messenger" but 178 times as "angel". Another place we find this same Greek word is 2 Corinthians 11, and is talking about Satan.

2 Corinthians 11:14

> *No wonder, for even Satan disguises himself as an **angel** of light.*

Keep in mind this is just one chapter earlier than chapter 12 about Paul's thorn. It could be that Paul's thorn in the flesh was an angel of Satan, what we would call an evil spirit, that would follow Paul around and stir up trouble everywhere he went. The overriding point here is—the thorn in the flesh was not from God, but Satan!

Another possibility was that the thorn in the flesh, the messenger of Satan, was a person. This would have been a legalistic Jew, called a *Judaizer*, who stirred up trouble in Paul's ministry by trying to convince people that they must be circumcised and follow all the Jewish laws and traditions in order to find favor with God.

Acts 13:50

> *But the Jewish leaders incited the God-fearing women of high standing and the leading men of the city. They stirred up persecution against Paul and Barnabas, and expelled them from their region.*

They would slander Paul and discredit him and his message. The book of Galatians was written by Paul to address this issue of people stirring up trouble.

Galatians 1:7

> *There are some who are disturbing you and want to distort the gospel of Christ*

Paul addressed false apostles who were causing trouble.

2 Corinthians 11:13

> *For such men are false apostles, deceitful workers, disguising themselves as apostles of Christ.*

These false apostles and deceitful workers were actually working for Satan himself and were considered to be his servants.

2 Corinthians 11:15

> *Therefore it is not surprising if **his servants** also disguise themselves as servants of righteousness*

That kind of sounds like chapter 12's "messenger of Satan." Therefore, Paul's thorn was either a person or an evil spirit sent by Satan to constantly harass and trouble Paul. Personally, I lean toward Paul's thorn being an evil spirit sent to constantly harass and stir up trouble wherever Paul went.

An evil spirit would be called an "angel" of Satan? Yes. Notice:

Matthew 25:41

> *Then He will also say to those on His left, 'Depart from Me, accursed ones, into the eternal fire which has been prepared for **the devil and his angels.**'*

Evil spirits are called the devil's angels. So "an angel of Satan" would be an evil spirit.

Either way, person or evil spirit, what did this messenger of Satan do to Paul?

To torment me

2 Corinthians 12:7

> *There was given me a thorn in the flesh, a messenger of Satan **to torment me.***

Now doesn't that sound just like God, to torment one of His beloved children (I'm being facetious here)?

It is nonsensical to believe that God would call a man to be an apostle with a revelation of Jesus Christ, and then hamstring him and slow him down from preaching that gospel by tormenting him with sickness.

The NASB says "torment me", the NKJV says "to buffet me." It is the Greek word, *kolaphizō*, which means "to strike with the fist." Besides being used here, *kolaphizō* is used four other times (Matthew 26:67,68; Mark 14:65; 1 Corinthians 4:11; and 1 Peter 2:19,20). In every one of those instances the word is used in the context of persecution. It is therefore consistent and logical to believe when it's used here in 2 Corinthians 12:7, that it means the exact same thing. We'll confirm this shortly in verse 10.

Paul's thorn in the flesh was either an angel of Satan, an evil spirit, or a person, sent to constantly buffet, strike with the fist, and torment Paul with constant persecution, to minimize his popularity and decrease his gospel effectiveness. And the bigger the proclaimer, the bigger the persecution.

Power is perfected in weakness

2 Corinthians 12:9

*And He has said to me, "My grace is sufficient for you, for power is perfected in **weakness**."*

"Weakness" in the Greek language can mean one of two things: weakness or sickness. So, was Paul referring to weakness or sickness in his life? After all, many pastors and teachers say that Paul's thorn in the flesh was sickness. To answer that question, we must look at the passage itself, keeping it in context. Notice the very next verse, verse 10, because it gives the answer.

2 Corinthians 12:10

*Therefore I am well content with **weaknesses**, with **insults**, with **distresses**, with **persecutions**, with **difficulties**, for Christ's sake; for when I am **weak**, then I am strong.*

He doesn't mention sickness in that verse at all. It tells us right here in the verse the nature of the suffering the devil (through an evil spirit or person) was causing in Paul's life—weakness, insults, distress, persecutions, and difficulties. Sickness is not mentioned! If Paul's thorn in the flesh was a sickness, wouldn't he have mentioned it? The things he names are all related to constant harassment through persecution.

It's as if the devil was saying to him, "You think you're so big and popular Paul, you think you're going to succeed in spreading the gospel? Watch this...BAM!" And then Satan sends one of his servants to stir up persecution in one man's life at an unprecedented level. To get a sense of the degree that this happened in Paul's life, we should read just a few chapters back in 2 Corinthians.

2 Corinthians 4:7-11

But we have this treasure in earthen vessels (a reference to weakness), **so that the surpassing greatness of the power will be of God** *and not from ourselves; we are afflicted in every way, but not crushed; perplexed, but not despairing; persecuted, but not forsaken; struck down, but not destroyed; always carrying about in the body the dying of Jesus, so that the life of Jesus also may be manifested in our body. For we who live are constantly being delivered over to death for Jesus' sake, so that the life of Jesus also may be manifested in our mortal flesh.*

Sickness is not mentioned once, it's all about persecution. And notice that Paul makes the very same connection between his weakness and God's power to get him through all the persecution and harassment—"so that the surpassing greatness of the power will be from God." Remember 2 Corinthians 12:9, "My power is perfected in weakness." Paul here is referring to the same thing.

One chapter before the chapter on Paul's thorn we have another list of what the Apostle Paul went through.

2 Corinthians 11:22-28

Are they Hebrews? So am I. Are they Israelites? So am I. Are they descendants of Abraham? So am I. Are they servants of Christ?—I speak as if insane—I more so; in far more labors, in far more imprisonments, beaten times without number, often in danger of death. Five times I received from the Jews thirty-nine lashes. Three times I was beaten with rods, once I was stoned, three times I was shipwrecked, a night and a day I have spent in the deep. I have been on frequent journeys, in dangers from rivers, dangers from robbers, dangers from my countrymen, dangers from the Gentiles, dangers in the city, dangers in the wilderness, dangers on the sea, dangers among false brethren; I have been in labor and hardship, through many sleepless nights, in hunger and thirst, often without food, in cold and exposure. Apart from such external things, there is the daily pressure on me of concern for all the churches.

Notice "such external things," not internal sickness, it was external persecution and adversity. In this list, sickness is not mentioned one time. The list is all about the persecution and distress he went through for proclaiming the gospel. Let me remind you of the context of Paul's thorn in the flesh from 2 Corinthians 12:10:

2 Corinthians 12:10

*Therefore I am well content with weaknesses, with insults, with **distresses**, with **persecutions**, with **difficulties**, for Christ's sake; for when I am weak, then I am strong.*

If we interpret 2 Corinthians 12 in context, Paul's thorn in the flesh was not sickness, but a person or evil spirit assigned to continually stir up persecution against him everywhere he went.

Didn't Paul refer to his sickness in Galatians?

To bolster the case that Paul's thorn in the flesh was a sickness, pastors and teachers will reference something Paul said in the book of Galatians.

Galatians 4:13-15

*But you know that it was because of a bodily **illness** that I preached the gospel to you the first time; and that which was a trial to you in **my bodily condition** you did not despise or loathe, but you received me as an angel of God, as Christ Jesus Himself. Where then is that sense of blessing you had? For I bear you witness that, if possible, you **would have plucked out your eyes and given them to me**.*

"You see, right there Paul admitted that he had an illness, a bodily condition, an eye condition!"

I believe the translators took some real liberties to translate this *illness* and *bodily condition*. I realize other translations say the same thing, but the word is "infirmity", which can be translated one of two ways, *weakness* or *sickness*. The word used in the King James is "infirmity".

The NKJV:

> *You know that because of **physical infirmity** I preached the gospel to you **at the first**. And **my trial which was in my flesh** you did not despise or reject, but you received me as an angel of God, even as Christ Jesus. What then was the blessing you enjoyed? For I bear you witness that, if possible, you would have plucked out your own eyes and given them to me.*

Here the word "infirmity" is used, not "illness." There is a big difference. The word "infirmity" in the Greek is *astheneia*. This Greek word means one of two things: weakness or sickness.

How does one determine whether it should be translated "weakness" or "sickness"? As always, we must carefully look at the context of the verse, and the events the verse is referring to.

The key to understanding Galatians 4:13 is to notice the three words, "at the first" (NKJV) or "the first time" (NASB). What is that referring to? Answer: It's referring to the first time Paul travelled to Galatia and preached there.

The book of Galatians was written to those living in the province of Galatia. That province had four principle cities: Antioch (of Pisidia), Lystra, Iconium, and Derbe. What happened when the Apostle Paul first went to those cities? This will give us the clue on whether Paul's condition was a weakness or sickness. Acts 14 tells the story (and this is critical to accurately understanding Galatians 4:13-15).

Acts 14:1-22 (Here I'm giving the main points of the passage)

> *In Iconium they entered the synagogue of the Jews*
>
> *A large number of people believed*
>
> *The Jews who disbelieved stirred up the minds of the Gentiles and embittered them against the brethren*
>
> *But the people of the city were divided; and some sided with the Jews, and some with the apostles*
>
> *An attempt was made by both the Gentiles and the Jews with their rulers, **to mistreat and to stone them***

> *They ... fled to the cities of Lycaonia, Lystra and Derbe*
>
> *Jews came from Antioch and Iconium, and having won over the crowds, they **stoned Paul and dragged him out of the city, supposing him to be dead.***
>
> *But while the disciples stood around him, he got up and entered the city.*
>
> *They returned to Lystra and to Iconium and to Antioch, strengthening the souls of the disciples, encouraging them to continue in the faith, and saying, "Through **many tribulations** (in context, persecution) we must enter the kingdom of God."*

What happened to Paul when he went to Galatia "the first time"? Answer: He was stoned to death and dragged out of the city! Being stoned to death and then dragged a good distance tends to make a person weak! It didn't make him sick, it made him weak!

In context, in Galatians 4:13, when it says, *You know that because of <u>physical infirmity</u> I preached the gospel to you <u>at the first</u>,* knowing that the Greek word can either mean weakness or sickness, it should be obvious now that the correct translation would have better been translated *weakness*, not illness or sickness.

Notice how this same Greek word, *astheneia*, is translated in Romans.

Romans 8:26

> *In the same way the Spirit also helps our **weakness**; for we do not know how to pray as we should, but the Spirit Himself intercedes for us with groanings too deep for words.*

The translators translated *astheneia* as "weakness" here but took some real creative liberty to translate it as "illness" in Galatians 4:13, even knowing that the key to understanding the verse was the story from Acts 14 which clearly gives the context.

The Berean Literal Bible of Galatians 4:13 says:

Galatians 4:13

> *Now you know that in **weakness of the flesh** I proclaimed the gospel the first time to you.*

71

That's a better translation. Paul refers to this weakness in 2 Corinthians 11:30 after listing all he went through with persecution.

2 Corinthians 11:30

*If I have to boast, I will boast of what pertains to my **weakness**.*

Now this makes perfect sense seeing in scripture all that Paul went through. At no time does it ever mention sickness. Paul's thorn in the flesh therefore was persecution, not sickness. Paul states:

2 Timothy 3:12

Indeed, all who desire to live godly in Christ Jesus will be persecuted.

My grace is sufficient

2 Corinthians 12:8-9

*Concerning this I implored the Lord three times that it might leave me. And He has said to me, "**My grace is sufficient for you**, for power is perfected in weakness." Most gladly, therefore, I will rather boast about my **weaknesses**, so that the power of Christ may dwell in me.*

Notice, "weaknesses," not "sickness." Paul requested the Lord to take away this thorn in the flesh that was causing all this persecution. God's answer:

*"My grace is sufficient for you, for power is perfected in **weakness**."*

Again, notice "weakness," not "sickness."

In other words, God said, "Paul, My grace and power will see you through these hardships. When you are weak, I show Myself strong in your life."

Persecution is the only kind of suffering (other than physical death) that believers in Christ are NOT redeemed from.

1 Peter 2:19-20

For this finds favor, if for the sake of conscience toward God a person bears up under sorrows when suffering unjustly. For what credit is there if, when you sin and are harshly treated, you endure it with patience? But if when you do what is right and suffer for it you patiently endure it, this finds favor with God.

We've been redeemed from sickness and disease, but we are not redeemed from persecution.

God specifically told Paul that his ministry would be marked by persecution. Notice what the Lord said to Ananias regarding Paul, when Paul first got saved.

Acts 9:15,16

*Go, for he is a chosen instrument of Mine, to bear My name before the Gentiles and kings and the sons of Israel; for **I will show him how much he must suffer for My name's sake**.*

Jesus, the Alpha and Omega, knowing the beginning from the end, saw how much Paul would suffer for the gospel. But, the Lord told Paul that His grace would be sufficient for him in the midst of hardship and persecution. Notice what Paul said in 1 Timothy 3:

1 Timothy 3:10-11

*Now you followed my teaching, conduct, purpose, faith, patience, love, perseverance, **persecutions, and sufferings**, such as happened to me at Antioch, at Iconium and at Lystra (the cities in Galatia); what **persecutions I endured**, and **out of them all the Lord rescued me**!*

Notice the nature of the sufferings, "persecutions."

God's grace was sufficient! God's grace enabled Paul to endure. God's grace rescued Paul out of them all! We need to drop this idea that Paul's thorn in the flesh was a sickness given to him by God, and that God's grace helped Paul endure this sickness. It just doesn't square with scripture.

CHAPTER 9

What About Job?

Just like Paul's thorn in the flesh, the story of Job has caused many people to believe that God is behind their suffering. You'll hear Job quoted at funerals, especially Job 1:21.

Job 1:21

The Lord gave and the Lord has taken away. Blessed be the name of the Lord.

Job is used to promote the idea that God allows Satan to hammer away at you just to prove what mettle (mettle = "courage to carry on") you're made of. It's written, according to some, to show us how to be patient during suffering, suffering which God has designed for some divine strategic purpose. There's no question that trusting God in the midst of suffering is a good thing. But the question I will endeavor to answer is...is it true that God caused Job to suffer or...have we missed something?

What's interesting to me is that in the last chapter of the book, God restored back to Job twofold everything that he lost in the first chapter of the book.

Job 42:10

The Lord restored the fortunes of Job when he prayed for his friends, and the Lord increased all that Job had twofold.

Chapter 1 and Chapter 42 are bookends with commonality. There are some mysterious connections between Chapter 1 and Chapter 42. What are they?

If God was the one who caused Job to lose it all, and then in the end gave it all back twofold, we're left with some head-scratching questions:

- Did Job mess up somewhere to warrant this open door to suffering?
- If not, why did his suffering occur?
- Was it God or Satan who did this?
- If God did it, what's the strategy behind taking it all away and the giving it all back in the end? Was it just to prove something to Satan? Was it so God could find out what Job was made of? If God knows the end from the beginning, wouldn't He know that already?
- If Satan did it, why did God allow it?
- What is the overall lesson we are to learn from Job?

One thing to keep in mind when we interpret the book of Job is that we must always interpret the Old Testament through the lens of the New Testament, not vice versa. This is crucial. When we look at Job through what we come to understand about God's character in the New Testament as seen in the life of Jesus Christ, what truth do we glean?

I won't spend much time on what is said between chapters 1 and 2 and chapter 42. These chapters contain a discussion between Job and his four friends; Eliphaz, Bildad, Zophar, and eventually, Elihu. The reason I don't want to cover these four men's ramblings is because they are four steams of consciousness that, in the end, are all said by God to be in error, including Job's.

Job's main point in defending himself was: "This is God doing this to me for no particular reason. God does this type of thing when He wants to." But God rebuked Job and told him that what he said wasn't right.

Job 38:1-2

Then the Lord answered Job out of the whirlwind and said, "Who is this that darkens counsel by words without knowledge?"

Job 40:1-4

Then the Lord said to Job, "Will the faultfinder contend with the Almighty? Let him who reproves God answer it." Then Job

> *answered the Lord and said, "Behold, I am insignificant; what can I reply to You? I lay my hand on my mouth."*

Job's four friends' main point was: "Job, this is God doing this to you in judgment because you've committed wickedness of some kind." (Job 4:7-11) But God rebuked Job's friends and told them that what they said about God wasn't right either.

Job 42:7

> *It came about after the Lord had spoken these words to Job, that the Lord said to Eliphaz the Temanite, "My wrath is kindled against you and against your two friends, because you have not spoken of Me what is right as My servant Job has.*

"You have not spoken of Me what is right as My servant Job has" is a reference to verses 1 through 6, where Job repented about the wrong things he had said about God.

Job 42:1-6

> *1 Then Job answered the Lord and said,*
>
> *2 "I know that You can do all things, and that no purpose of Yours can be thwarted.*
>
> *3 'Who is this that hides counsel without knowledge (here Job quotes God's question to him)?' Therefore I have declared that which I did not understand, things too wonderful for me, which I did not know.*
>
> *4 Hear, now, and I will speak; I will ask You, and You instruct me.*
>
> *5 I have heard of You by the hearing of the ear; but now my eye sees You;*
>
> *6 therefore I retract, and I repent in dust and ashes.*

Since neither Job nor his friends were speaking about God what was right, I won't take time to comment on it. Chapters 1, 2 and 42 therefore become our focus.

At the end of the book, God rebukes Job's friends and has them go to Job so he can do a sacrifice and pray for them to assuage God's anger.

Job 42:8

> *Now therefore, take for yourselves seven bulls and seven rams, and go to My servant Job, and offer up a burnt offering for yourselves, and My servant Job will pray for you. For I will accept him so that I may not do with you according to your folly, because you have not spoken of Me what is right, as My servant Job has."*

Chapters 1 and 42 have striking similarities. Both chapters talk about a sacrifice and prayer followed by consequences that affected the material and physical. In chapter 1, Job loses everything and in chapter 42, he gains it all back twofold.

Even without looking at the details, it would seem there was something wrong in the sacrifice and prayer in chapter 1, and something right and redemptive in the sacrifice and prayer in chapter 42. So, let's look at chapter 1 and take note of some of the details.

Job 1:1-5

> *1   There was a man in the land of Uz whose name was Job; and that man was blameless, upright, fearing God and turning away from evil.*
>
> *2   Seven sons and three daughters were born to him.*
>
> *3   His possessions also were 7,000 sheep, 3,000 camels, 500 yoke of oxen, 500 female donkeys, and very many servants; and that man was the greatest of all the men of the east.*
>
> *4   His sons used to go and hold a feast in the house of each one on his day (probably birthday), and they would send and invite their three sisters to eat and drink (vs 13 – wine) with them.*
>
> *5   When the days of feasting had completed their cycle, Job would send and **consecrate them**, rising up early in the morning and **offering burnt offerings** according to the number of them all; for Job said, "**Perhaps** my sons have sinned and cursed God in their hearts." Thus Job **did continually**.*

First of all, when it says that Job was "blameless, upright, fearing God and turning away from evil", it couldn't mean that he was perfect and sinless, because of all people born on this earth, only Jesus Christ was sinless (Hebrews 4:15; 1 Peter 2:22). Therefore, it would mean that Job, although not without sin, feared God, followed Him the best he could, and stayed away from evil.

There are three important things to note here in Chapter 1.

1. Job offered sacrifices for sin without being commanded by God to do so. Compare this with chapter 42 where he offered a sacrifice in obedience to God's command.

2. Job wasn't even certain his sons and daughters had, in fact, committed any sin, for he said, "**Perhaps** my sons have sinned and cursed God in their hearts." The word "perhaps" indicates that Job didn't know for sure, but was fearful they did.

3. Job did this continually, so this wasn't a one-off, it was a fearful habit.

Job was acting in fear here, not faith and obedience to God, and again, he did this continually. I believe Job's acting in fear in this way repeatedly was the thing that opened the door for Satan to attack him so viciously.

In the end, God rebukes both Job and his friends, and after Job's prayer, offering and sacrifice (a sacrifice done in obedience and faith), Job's fortunes are restored twofold. The error of Job 1 is corrected in Job 42. Let's compare the similar elements between the first and last chapters of Job.

Job 1   **Job 42**

Job offered sacrifices for sin for his sons and daughters without being commanded by God to do so.	Job offered sacrifice for sin for his friends in obedience to God's command.
Wasn't sure his sons and daughters had sinned.	Was sure his friends had sinned (God told Job that).
Did this repeatedly.	Did this one time.
Was acting in fear.	Was acting in faith.
Job loses everything.	Job gains everything back twofold.

If what I just presented was not true, someone would have to explain to me the whole purpose of verses 1-5 (Job's repeated sacrifices based out of fear for his children) for our understanding of the book of Job. Why else would God put that in there if those verses were totally insignificant and irrelevant? Just observing chapters 1 and 42 as bookends with these similar elements helps us to understand the 'why' of it all.

Faith is of God, fear is of Satan. Fear is the opposite of faith. Just like faith releases God to work on our behalf (Mark 5:34, Luke 17:19 – "Your faith has made you whole"), fear releases Satan to work against us and attack us.

Job 3:25

For what I fear comes upon me, and what I dread befalls me.

Satan needs four primary open doors to get into someone's life:

1) A lifestyle of intentional sin.
2) Ignorance.
3) Unforgiveness.
4) Fear.

I believe it's clear that Job was operating in fear, not faith and obedience.

Who did this to Job?

Job thought that it was God who caused these attacks and suffering.

Job 1:21

80

> *The Lord gave and the Lord has taken away. Blessed be the name of the Lord.*

Why did Job think this? The answer is—because Job knew nothing about Satan or a personal devil who, in the words of John 10:10, "steals, kills and destroys".

Not one time in the book of Job does Job or any of his friends bring up the possibility that these attacks were caused by God's arch enemy, the devil. Satan is mentioned by the author of the book of Job (author unknown) who narrates the story, but never by Job or his friends.

It's easy for us in the New Testament to understand the reality of Satan and spiritual warfare, but Job knew nothing about this. Consequently, Job's only point of reference was God, and that's whom he affixed the cause for his suffering.

But we don't have to wonder who did this to Job, plainly, it was Satan.

Job 2:7

> *Then **Satan** went out from the presence of the LORD and smote Job with sore boils from the sole of his foot to the crown of his head.*

Did God commission Satan to afflict Job?

At first glance, it would seem like God, although He didn't do this to Job directly, actively commissioned Satan to do it. We call this "the Mafia theory". The godfather of the mafia didn't actually commit the murder, it was done by a hitman, but everybody knows who was behind the murder. And in our judicial system, the boss who ordered it is just as guilty as the hitman who pulled the trigger. The same kind of thinking happens with many people when they think about Job's suffering.

In the book of Job, so people think, Satan did it but God was behind it. It's like someone with a mad dog on a leash who unhooks the dog and lets him go free to attack someone. The dog's owner could always exclaim, "Wait, it's the dog that bit you, not me!", with the understandable retort, "Yeah, but you let the dog off the leash!"

This erroneous idea comes from Job 2, so we need to examine it carefully.

Job 2:1-7

> *1   Again there was a day when the sons of God came to present themselves before the Lord, and Satan also came among them to present himself before the Lord.*
>
> *2   The Lord said to Satan, "Where have you come from?" Then Satan answered the Lord and said, "From roaming about on the earth and walking around on it."*
>
> *3   The Lord said to Satan, "**Have you considered My servant Job**? For there is no one like him on the earth, a blameless and upright man fearing God and turning away from evil. And he still holds fast his integrity, although you incited Me against him to ruin him without cause."*
>
> *4   Satan answered the Lord and said, "Skin for skin! Yes, all that a man has he will give for his life.*
>
> *5   However, put forth Your hand now, and touch his bone and his flesh; he will curse You to Your face."*
>
> *6   So the Lord said to Satan, "Behold, he is in your power, only spare his life."*
>
> *7   Then Satan went out from the presence of the Lord and smote Job with sore boils from the sole of his foot to the crown of his head.*

No one fully understands why the angels and Satan presented themselves before the Lord here in Chapter 1. Biblical scholars speculate that there was an assembly of angels that came before God's throne, probably to give an account of their activities. But for whatever reason, both angels and Satan present themselves before the Lord for a little chat.

Then God asked Satan a question, and I'll paraphrase, "So Satan, what have you been up to lately?" Was this because God didn't know what Satan was up to? Hardly. God knows everything. So why did God ask Satan this? It's because God is making Satan accountable to Him by drawing Satan out, forcing him to answer.

Satan's response to God's question was, "I've been roaming around the earth." Why would Satan be roaming around the earth?

What was he up to? It sounds like he was planning and scheming something. There's only one reason Satan would do this.

1 Peter 5:8

*Be of sober spirit, be on the alert. Your adversary, the devil, prowls around like a roaring lion, **seeking someone to devour**.*

That's Satan's mission on earth, to roam around and seek someone to devour.

John 10:10

The thief comes only to steal and kill and destroy.

Then God asked Satan a second question.

Job 2:3

The Lord said to Satan, "Have you considered My servant Job? For there is no one like him on the earth, a blameless and upright man fearing God and turning away from evil. And he still holds fast his integrity, although you incited Me against him to ruin him without cause."

The same question was posed by God in Job 1:8.

Job 1:8

The Lord said to Satan, "Have you considered My servant Job? For there is no one like him on the earth, a blameless and upright man, fearing God and turning away from evil."

Two points here:

First, Satan tried to incite God to afflict Job. God didn't succumb to this because He refused to be manipulated by Satan and didn't have any cause to do so. God does sometimes afflict the wicked in judgment (reference the flood and Sodom and Gomorrah), but not His righteous ones!

Second, God rhetorically asks Satan, "Have you considered My servant, Job, there's no one like him?"

There are two ways to look at God's question to Satan:

1. "Have you considered My servant, Job, because if you haven't, you should consider attacking him because he's a worthy person, one of My finest."
   - Friends, that doesn't align with the character of God or make sense!

2. God asked this question like a parent asking a child if they've stolen cookies from the cookie jar. The parent knows full well that the child has done this but asks, "Have you eaten any cookies from the cookie jar?" in order to draw from them an answer for the sake of accountability.

So God asked Satan, "Have you considered My servant, Job, as you've roamed around the earth?" God knew full well that Satan had, but He asked this rhetorically to let him know He was onto him.[27] Remember, God was most likely calling the angels and Satan's actions into account during this assembly.

In verse 4, Satan says, "Skin for skin! Yes, all that a man has he will give for his life." What Satan meant here was, "Skin for skin", or in other words, it's a *quid pro quo*, "It's an even exchange! You protect Job and in return he serves You. Of course Job will serve and obey You!"

Then Satan said to God in verse 5, "However, put forth Your hand now, and touch his bone and his flesh; he will curse You to Your face." Satan again tries to incite God to afflict His servant Job. God does not take orders from the devil. Neither does He allow Himself to be manipulated by the devil.

In verse 6 God replied to Satan, "Behold, he is in your power, only spare his life." This could mean one of two things:

1) "I, God, actively and intentionally give you, Satan, permission to afflict Job, just don't kill him. I'm taking you off the leash so you can sic him!"

or

2) "Behold (look!), Job is already in your power because he's been operating in fear and opened the door, you just didn't

realize it. Look, he's in your power already, but I will not allow you to kill him."

I submit to you that #2 is the better interpretation to what God was saying to Satan in verse 6.

The very next verse, verse 7, says, "Then Satan went out from the presence of the Lord and smote Job."

God was NOT unhooking Satan off the leash so that he could attack one of His precious saints who was upright, feared Him and turned away from evil! He was pointing out to Satan that Job was already in his power because of an open door caused by Job's continual fear sacrifices, none of which were commanded by God.

Some people will say that Job didn't think it was God doing this to him because of what of what's said in Job 1:22.

Job 1:22 NIV

In all this, Job did not sin by charging God with wrongdoing.

The King James Version says, "In all this Job sinned not, nor charged God foolishly."

The fact is, Job DID blame God for what happened, but he didn't do this because of malice, ill intent or foolish anger. He thought God was behind it, but that God wasn't doing this to Job as an act of wrongdoing or evil.

But there's no doubt, Job thought God was the one doing this to him. Here are Job's famous words.

Job 13:15

Though He slay me, I will hope in Him.

Job 2:9-10

*Then his wife said to him, "Do you still hold fast your integrity? Curse God and die!" But he said to her, "You speak as one of the foolish women speaks. **Shall we indeed accept good from God and not accept adversity?**" In all this Job did not sin with his lips.*

Job most assuredly believed God was the one behind his suffering. But Job didn't accuse God of evil or rail against Him.

Some people are confused because of how Job 42:11 reads:

Job 42:11

> *Then all his brothers and all his sisters and all who had known him before came to him, and they ate bread with him in his house; and they consoled him and comforted him **for all the adversities that the Lord had brought on him**. And each one gave him one piece of money, and each a ring of gold.*

But this needs to be interpreted in light of what we know from the rest of the book of Job. We know that it was Satan who did this to Job (Job 2:7). We also know that although God allowed it to happen to Job, the Lord was very upset with both Job and his friends for accusing Him being behind the attacks. Because both of those things are true, we must interpret Job 42:11 as, "for all the adversities that the Lord ALLOWED to be brought on him." No other way of interpreting this verse will maintain harmony and congruency with the rest of the book.

Although Job accused God of doing this to him, an accusation he later got reprimanded by God for, he still maintained that his actions had nothing to do with it.

Job 32:1

> *Then these three men ceased answering Job, because he was righteous in his own eyes.*

Elihu rebuked Job because of his self-righteous attitude.

Job 35:2

> *Do you think this is according to justice? Do you say, "My righteousness is more than God's?"*

Job was a good man, an upright man, who feared God and turned away from evil (Job 1:1), but he wasn't perfect, and he still sinned from time to time.

Interpret Job through Jesus Christ

We must interpret the Old Testament through the lens of the New Testament (more on this in the next chapter). This means we must interpret Job through observing the life of Jesus Christ. And what do we see Jesus doing in the New Testament?

- Healing people, not making them sick
- Setting people free, not oppressing them
- Giving to people, not subtracting or taking away from them
- Destroying the works of the devil (1 John 3:8), not using the devil to make people suffer

As we look at Jesus, we cannot, we MUST not believe that God makes people suffer.

What we have in the New Testament that Job didn't have

Keep in mind that in the New Testament we have numerous blessings and benefits that Job did not have:

1. An understanding of the devil.
2. An understanding of spiritual warfare.
3. Being transformed as new creations in Christ (2 Corinthians 5:17).
4. The written Word of God for our instruction.
5. Endued with the power of the Holy Spirit from on high (Luke 24:49, Acts 1:8).
6. The name above all names, the name of Jesus (Philippians 2:9).
7. Authority over the devil (Luke 10:19).
8. The right and authority to resist Satan (James 4:7) so that he will flee from us.

For Job to have none of those things, yet be described as a man who was blameless, upright, fearing God and turning away from evil, is most impressive.

The lesson we are to learn from Job

Like everything in the Old Testament, we are to learn from it.

1 Corinthians 10:6, 11

> *Now these things happened as examples for us ... Now these things happened to them as an example, and they were written for our instruction, upon whom the ends of the ages have come.*

Romans 15:4

> *For whatever was written in earlier times was written for our instruction, so that through perseverance and the encouragement of the Scriptures we might have hope.*

So, what is the lesson we are to learn from the book of Job? In James' letter, we are told what we're to learn from Job's story.

James 5:11

> *We count those blessed who endured. You have heard of the endurance of Job and have seen the outcome of the Lord's dealings, that the Lord is full of compassion and is merciful.*

The two main lessons from Job are:

1.   Endurance based on trust.

Job never gave up trusting and loving God, and this trust enabled him to endure. In the end, he was blessed more than he ever had been before.

2.   God's compassion and mercy.

It's God's compassion and mercy that turned Job's captivity around, blessing him with twice as much as he had before. It was God's compassion and mercy that led Job to the place of repentance and restoration.

And, if you still believe that you MUST be like *poor ole Job*, then make sure you trust God, act in faith and allow God to give you back twice as much as you lost!

CHAPTER 10

Everything Happens for a Reason

One of the most common replies when hearing about suffering is, "Well, everything happens for a reason." This of course causes the sufferer to wonder what that reason is. It also implies two things: 1) God is causing it, and 2) there's some divine strategic reason for it. Wrestling with those two implications could drive a person nuts, not to mention the induced load of guilt it normally brings.

What I find intriguing is that when asked if they know God's reason for their suffering, almost all people say 'no.' What? Are you kidding? God is making you suffer for a reason but He hasn't told you the reason? How would you grade a teacher who is teaching you something but you have no idea what he or she is teaching you?

In reality, "everything happens for reason" is just something people say and there is no scriptural basis for it. It's something a perceived smart person said one time and then been repeated ever since. It's similar to "you should drink 10 glasses of water each day to be healthy." I'll guarantee you that one perceived smart person said that one time and it's been repeated ever since. But it's just not true. Really, who can do that and still keep a job?

Just like Paul's thorn and Job, if you've been a Christian for any length of time, you have heard pastors and teachers quote scripture verses that seem to support the idea that God is the one behind people's suffering for some cosmic reason. In this chapter I want to touch on these verses and hopefully shed some light on them, or at least make you think about them in a new way.

I'll do this in two sections; the first dealing with verses saying that God makes people suffer, and the second covering verses about God's sovereignty and that He does whatever He pleases.

God inflicts suffering?

The first category deals with God inflicting suffering on people. At first glance, it appears that God's in the habit of doing this.

1 Peter 5:10

After you have suffered for a little while, the God of all grace, who called you to His eternal glory in Christ, will Himself perfect, confirm, strengthen and establish you.

To interpret the verse correctly, we must look at the context by noting the previous verse, verse 9.

1 Peter 5:9

But resist him, firm in your faith, knowing that the same experiences of suffering are being accomplished by your brethren who are in the world.

This is talking about resisting Satan who is causing God's children to suffer PERSECTUION. The whole context is persecution. Only look at the previous chapter to see this.

1 Peter 4:12-16

12   Beloved, do not be surprised at the fiery ordeal among you, which comes upon you for your testing, as though some strange thing were happening to you;

13   but to the degree that you share the sufferings of Christ, keep on rejoicing, so that also at the revelation of His glory you may rejoice with exultation.

14   If you are reviled for the name of Christ, you are blessed, because the Spirit of glory and of God rests on you.

15   Make sure that none of you suffers as a murderer, or thief, or evildoer, or a troublesome meddler;

16   but if anyone suffers as a Christian, he is not to be ashamed, but is to glorify God in this name.

So the subject is persecution, and 1 Peter 5:10 is telling us that in the midst of persecution for being believers in Christ, God will perfect, confirm, strengthen and establish us. But He is NOT the one causing it.

As stated previously, there are two things that we are NOT redeemed from as far as the work of the cross ... persecution and physical death.

Inevitably, people bring up Deuteronomy 32:39 as proof God makes people suffer.

Deuteronomy 32:39

> *See now that I, I am He, and there is no god besides Me;* ***it is I*** ***who put to death*** *and give life.* ***I have wounded*** *and it is I who heal, and there is no one who can deliver from My hand.*

It's pretty clear, isn't it? God wounds and puts to death. And to that I would respond, "Yes, He does." But the question is...who?

To answer that question, it would help to read the verses following verse 39:

Deuteronomy 32:40-43

> *40   Indeed, I lift up My hand to heaven, and say, as I live forever,*
>
> *41   if I sharpen My flashing sword, and My hand takes hold on justice, I will render vengeance on My adversaries, and I will repay those who hate Me.*
>
> *42   I will make* ***My arrows*** *drunk with blood, and My sword will devour flesh, with the blood of the slain and the captives, from the long-haired leaders of* ***the enemy.'***
>
> *43   "Rejoice, O nations, with His people; for* ***He will avenge*** ***the blood of His servants****, and will* ***render vengeance on His*** ***adversaries****, and will atone for His land and His people."*

If you take verse 39 all by itself, it would be easy to think the Lord wounds and kills pretty much anybody for no particular reason. But when you look at verses 40-43, the context is clear— it's talking about God taking vengeance on behalf of His people against His enemies.

God has and will execute judgment on His enemies and upon wickedness. It would be error, however, to believe the Lord does this to His own dear children who are Christ-followers. Let's look at another one.

2 Kings 17:25

At the beginning of their living there, they did not fear the Lord; therefore the Lord sent lions among them which killed some of them.

Again, the context is clear, this was judgment against those who did not fear the Lord and by implication, committed evil.

Psalm 105:16

He called down famine on the land and destroyed all their supplies of food.

What's the context for God sending this famine? Let's read the next two verses.

Psalm 105:17-18

He sent a man before them, Joseph, who was sold as a slave. They afflicted his feet with fetters, he himself was laid in irons.

This is talking about Egypt, who oppressed Joseph, God's chosen man to deliver His people. In the midst of this famine, God raised up Joseph as a deliverer. Compare what we just read in Psalm 105:16 with Psalm 33:18,19:

Psalm 33:18-19

Behold, the eye of the Lord is on those who fear Him, on those who hope for His lovingkindness, to deliver their soul from death and to keep them alive in famine.

The truth about Psalm 105:16—the famine was sent to Israel's oppressors, Egypt, but the Lord blessed and kept His people alive during famine by providing food for them because of Joseph's position. Egypt didn't fear the Lord, but the Israelites did. Another reference that people use to promote the idea that God causes suffering is found in 1 Samuel 2.

1 Samuel 2:6-8

The LORD kills and makes alive; He brings down to Sheol and raises up. The LORD makes poor and rich; He brings low, He also exalts. He raises the poor from the dust, He lifts the needy from the ash heap to make them sit with nobles, and inherit a seat of honor; for the pillars of the earth are the LORD'S, and He set the world on them.

People will use this verse to make the case that the Lord kills people and makes them poor. But read the next two verses.

1 Samuel 2:9-10

*He keeps the feet of His godly ones, **but the wicked ones are silenced in darkness**; for not by might shall a man prevail. **Those who contend with the LORD will be shattered**; against them He will thunder in the heavens, the LORD **will judge** the ends of the earth; and He will give strength to His king, and will exalt the horn of His anointed.*

If we pay careful attention to the context, we see that it speaks of God's judgment, and the ones killed or made poor are the wicked and those who contend with Him, but God protects and blesses His godly ones.

Here is one of the most used verses to sell the idea that God causes suffering.

Exodus 4:11

The LORD said to him, "Who has made man's mouth? Or who makes him mute or deaf, or seeing or blind? Is it not I, the LORD?

God MAKES people mute, deaf and blind? Is that right? I have three main points to make regarding Exodus 4:11.

First, the backstory to this is that God called Moses to go to Pharaoh and speak to him. Moses recoiled and told God he couldn't do that because he wasn't a good speaker...that he wasn't great with words or fluent in speech.

Exodus 4:10

> *Then Moses said to the Lord, "Please, Lord, I have never been eloquent, neither recently nor in time past, nor since You have spoken to Your servant; for I am slow of speech and slow of tongue."*

Some even think Moses had somewhat of a speech impediment, although it doesn't say that. To whatever degree and for whatever reason, Moses wasn't great with words, and didn't want to be the one whom God sent to Pharaoh.

The Lord reacted to Moses with anger. It's as if God said to Moses, "I created all human beings, including you Moses! I made the deaf-mutes and I made those who hear; I made the blind and I made those who see. I can use you however I want! I can work around any defect or lack of ability you have!"

God was rebuking Moses for his lack of faith, and rhetorically asks, "Hey, who made man's mouth?" Does that mean that God contemplates each person upon their creation as to whether they should be born with a mouth or not? No! And it doesn't mean upon their creation they will be born blind or deaf by His sovereign and intentional decree.

Second, and more importantly, the wording from the Hebrew (the Old Testament was written in Hebrew) is not the best here. Does the verse say:

1) "I make the deaf and mute, I make the seeing and the blind."

or

2) "I make them deaf and mute, I'm the one who makes them blind, I purposely made them with those defects"?

There's a big difference!

The New King James Version of Exodus 4:11 reads:

> *Who has made man's mouth? Or who makes the mute, the deaf, the seeing, or the blind? Have not I, the LORD?*

That is a huge difference from the New American Standard Bible. It doesn't say the Lord intentionally made them mute, deaf or blind; it says the Lord made all people—the seeing and those who don't see, He made the deaf and those who hear.

If we look at the literal Hebrew, the direct object "him" is not used in the verse at all. It doesn't say "Who made *him* deaf, mute and blind." It says "Who made the deaf, mute and blind." Again, big difference.

Here's the literal Hebrew:

> *And the Lord said unto him, "Who hath made man's mouth, or who maketh the dumb, or deaf, or the seeing, or the blind? Have not I the Lord?*

It doesn't say "Who made him dumb." It says, "Who makes the dumb, or deaf, or the seeing, or the blind?"

So, in this verse, God isn't addressing the cause of deafness or blindness, but Moses' lack of faith and unwillingness to go as God's spokesman.

Third, we must not interpret the New Testament through the Old Testament; rather, we must interpret the Old Testament through what we see in the New Testament.

When we look at Jesus in the gospels, do we see Him making people sick, diseased or infirmed in any way? No! We see the complete opposite...Jesus healing, delivering making whole, and adding to their lives, not subtracting. When we look at Jesus we are seeing the very character of the Father. Notice what Jesus said.

John 14:9

> *He who has seen Me has seen the Father.*

To understand and grasp the character of the Father, just look at the Son, Jesus Christ.

Hebrews 1:3

> *And He (Jesus) is the radiance of His glory and the exact representation of His nature.*

Jesus was and is the exact representation of God's nature. And what did Jesus do? He healed and set people free from suffering, He did not put sickness, disease, disabilities, or poverty on people!

One time a leper came up to Jesus and asked Him if He was willing to heal him. This is the question that most people wonder about with God and their sickness—is God willing to heal me?

Matthew 8:1-3

> When Jesus came down from the mountain, large crowds followed Him. And a leper came to Him and bowed down before Him, and said, "Lord, **if You are willing**, You can make me clean." Jesus stretched out His hand and touched him, saying, "**I am willing**; be cleansed." And immediately his leprosy was cleansed.

The man asked a theological question, if Jesus was willing to heal him. Jesus settled his theology quickly, "I am willing!" And Jesus is willing today as well, because Jesus is the same yesterday, today and forever (Hebrews 13:8).

To use Exodus 4:11 as prooftext that God intentionally creates people deaf and blind doesn't line up with 1) what the verse is actually saying in the original Hebrew language no0r 2) the character of God as revealed through Jesus Christ.

In this first point, the issue isn't whether God has, in His justice, punished evil doers. Noah's flood along with Sodom and Gomorrah certainly are examples of God punishing wickedness. The issue is—does the Lord make people suffer who are NOT coming under judgment for their wickedness? And the answer to that is, no.

God does whatever He pleases

The first section dealt with "Does God inflict suffering?" The second point deals with God being sovereign and doing whatever He pleases, whatever He wills. Of course, that is true.

Job 23:13

> But He is unique and who can turn Him? And **what His soul desires, that He does**.

Psalm 135:6

> *The Lord does whatever pleases him, in the heavens and on the earth, in the seas and all their depths. (NIV)*

Isaiah 46:9-10

> *Remember the former things long past, for I am God, and there is no other; I am God, and there is no one like Me, declaring the end from the beginning, and from ancient times things which have not been done, saying, '**My purpose will be established, and I will accomplish all My good pleasure**'.*

Isaiah 14:27

> *For the Lord of hosts **has planned, and who can frustrate it**? And as for His stretched-out hand, **who can turn it back**?"*

There is no doubt, God is sovereign and does whatever He desires, and whatever He wills.

But, here is another question— is it ever God's desire or will to refrain from MAKING something happen and allow mankind to determine the outcome instead? In other words, God does whatever He desires, that's true, but what if God purposely limits Himself and allows mankind to make the choice?

Deuteronomy 30:15-16,19-20

> *See, I have set before you today life and prosperity, and death and adversity; ... I have set before you life and death, the blessing and the curse. So **choose life** in order that you may live, you and your descendants, by loving the LORD your God, by obeying His voice.*

God gives us choices! He does NOT make us do anything, He does not force us or go against our will. We can choose life, prosperity and blessing by obeying, or we can choose death and adversity by disobedience. Even though God desires us to obey, we have a choice. How do we reconcile that with the next two verses?

Psalm 103:19

> *The Lord has established His throne in the heavens, and <u>His sovereignty rules over all</u>.*

1 John 5:19

We know that we are of God, and that the whole world lies in the power of the evil one.

His sovereignty rules over all, but wait, the Bible also says that the whole world lies in the power of the evil one, or Satan (1 John 5:19). How can this be? Remember the definition of *sovereign*. There are different aspects of this word's definition.

Sovereign
- Supreme in authority
- Supreme in rank or power
- Unrestricted

God is supreme in authority, power and rank, but...He has chosen to restrict Himself temporarily in many cases and to a certain measured degree, allowing mankind to make choices, and additionally, for Satan to have a temporary and measured degree of powerful influence.

God's will and desires will always come to pass as far as His current and ultimate plan for the world and end-time events, but He does NOT micromanage every detail of what goes on here on planet earth, including our lives.

That's easy to prove. Did you sin in some fashion in the last seven days? Of course, we all did. Did God desire and will for you to sin? No, of course not. Well, there you go.

Part 3

Ten Reasons for Suffering

Chapter 11

Because We're Living in a Fallen World

The primary reason there is suffering in the world is because we're living in a fallen world, and we must assign blame for this to mankind, not God, for it was not God's will.

The Garden of Eden was perfect. Adam and Eve were created perfect. They had been given authority over all the earth and animals as under-rulers.

Genesis 1:26-28

> 26   Then God said, "Let Us make man in Our image, according to Our likeness; and **let them rule** over the fish of the sea and over the birds of the sky and over the cattle and over all the earth, and over every creeping thing that creeps on the earth."
>
> 27   God created man in His own image, in the image of God He created him; male and female He created them.
>
> 28   God blessed them; and God said to them, "Be fruitful and multiply, and **fill the earth, and subdue it; and rule over** the fish of the sea and over the birds of the sky and over every living thing that moves on the earth."

This authority handed over to mankind was a heavenly *power of attorney*. God handed over to mankind the authority to rule and make decisions. And, God would respect mankind's decisions.

Mankind had almost total freedom. Almost. They were told that they could eat from any tree in the Garden of Eden except for one, the *Tree of the Knowledge of Good and Evil*.

What's the big deal about the Tree of the Knowledge of Good and Evil? Why was that forbidden? The answer: Because God didn't want mankind to think, experience, have to make decisions about, or even be cognizant of evil. He wanted them to only know and experience good. Leave the whole evil thing alone!

Enter the scene, Satan, the tempter, and he sells Adam and Eve a line to seduce them into rebellion against God, which is the sin he personally committed long before this.

Genesis 3:1-6

> *1   Now the serpent was more crafty than any beast of the field which the Lord God had made. And he said to the woman, "Indeed, has God said, 'You shall not eat from any tree of the garden'?"*
>
> *2   The woman said to the serpent, "From the fruit of the trees of the garden we may eat;*
>
> *3   but from the fruit of the tree which is in the middle of the garden, God has said, 'You shall not eat from it or touch it, or you will die.'"*
>
> *4   The serpent said to the woman, "You surely will not die!*
>
> *5   For God knows that in the day you eat from it your eyes will be opened, and you will be like God, knowing good and evil."*
>
> *6   When the woman saw that the tree was good for food, and that it was a delight to the eyes, and that the tree was desirable to make one wise, she took from its fruit and ate; and she gave also to her husband with her, and he ate.*

It's what is called mankind's fall into sin, or for brevity, "the fall." Mankind fell from grace, fell from a love relationship with God Himself.

The temptation that Satan lured Adam and Eve with was that they would be like God, knowing good and evil. This was, in a sense, partially true because only God has the absolute right and authority to discern good and evil. In fact, the more we grow spiritually and become more like Christ, the more we mature, the better grasp we have on discerning good from evil.

Hebrews 5:14

> *For everyone who partakes only of milk is not accustomed to the word of righteousness, for he is an infant. But solid food is*

*for the mature, who because of practice **have their senses trained to discern good and evil**.*

Maturation develops an ever-increasing accurate sense of good and evil. Ultimate maturity (God), has the ultimate right to declare what is good and evil. So there is only one person who has the right to decide what is good and what is evil, and that is God Himself.

Satan's fall resulted from rebelling and trying to usurp God's authority (Isaiah 14:12-14). Now he was trying to seduce mankind to do the exact same thing. And he succeeded.

As a side note, mankind's main problem today is, just like Satan along with Adam and Eve, taking right/wrong, and good/evil, into their own hands. "Don't tell us what is sinful! We get to decide that!" "Don't impose your moral code on us!" That's why, without God, morality is a total farce, for there is no ultimate objective authority. There is no moral magnetic north to calibrate our moral compasses to.

As soon as mankind sinned, there exploded into Planet Earth a curse consisting of all manner of evil and subsequent suffering. And, it affected all of us from that moment forward.

Romans 5:12

Therefore, just as through one man sin entered into the world, and death through sin, and so death spread to all men.

It started with spiritual death (separation from God), then morphed into every kind of evil imaginable:

- hatred
- sickness and disease
- physical death
- poverty and lack
- mental illness and oppression
- physical and mental disabilities
- murder
- tragedy and calamity
- weather disasters
- accidents
- premature death
- anger and jealousy

- domination
- lust
- and all forms of sin

The moment Adam and Eve sinned, they signed over to Satan that power of attorney. Now Satan had a legal right to unleash all evil and suffering into the earth. Why didn't God just stop it? Answer: Because God respected His heavenly jurisprudence (system of law)! It was, if I can put it this way, a legal transaction in giving authority to man. And, it was a legal transaction in mankind giving it away to Satan. God would respect mankind's fateful decision.

Notice what Satan said to Jesus in the wilderness when taking Him up to the pinnacle of the temple and tempting Him.

Luke 4:5,6

*And he led Him up and showed Him all the kingdoms of the world in a moment of time. And the devil said to Him, "I will give You all this domain and its glory; **for it has been handed over to me**, and I give it to whomever I wish.*

"For it has been handed over to me," and Satan was telling the truth here. Power, not absolute power, for only God possesses that, but a measured degree of power was handed over from Adam and Eve to Satan. It was a legal transaction, for God had given them that authority, and their decision to sin resulted in forfeiting that authority over to Satan. No wonder even Jesus, when He walked this earth, said of Satan:

John 14:30

*I will not speak much more with you, for **the ruler of the world** is coming, and he has nothing in Me.*

Jesus referred to Satan as *the ruler of the world*. That will mess with your theology!

The curse, because of mankind's fall, is present here on earth. It's in the air. The only thing you need to do to experience the effects of the curse is to be born. Period. You don't have to do one thing wrong to experience it, it's just here.

Man was made in the image of God (Genesis 1:26), but the image of God in mankind has been marred ever since the fall. Even creation itself has been marred and affected by the curse, which is why we have natural evil. Prior to the fall there were no destructive earthquakes, hurricanes, tornados, tsunamis, fires or floods. Because of the fall, all of creation suffered and looks forward to the day of redemption, when all things are new.

Romans 8:19-22

> 19   For the anxious longing of the creation waits eagerly for the revealing of the sons of God.
>
> 20   For the creation was subjected to futility, not willingly, but because of Him who subjected it, in hope
>
> 21   that the creation itself also will be set free from its slavery to corruption into the freedom of the glory of the children of God.
>
> 22   For we know that the whole creation groans and suffers the pains of childbirth together until now.

But there is coming a day when, even this physical earth, will become brand new, delivered from its marred and corrupted state (Revelation 21:1). And there's coming a day when there will be no more sickness or disease, no more death, no more sorrow, and no more suffering (Revelation 21:4).

Until that time, there will be suffering—all a result of mankind's disobedience. Don't blame God, blame mankind, for in that moment of rebellion against God, Adam and Eve opened a floodgate of every form of evil and suffering. And because mankind was given legal power of attorney to rule the earth and make decisions, God was obligated to respect that decision, even with its evil consequences.

The good news is, after man sinned, (and in reality, even before man sinned, Revelation 13:8 – "the Lamb who was slain from the creation of the world." NIV), God had a plan to turn things around. Genesis 3 is the story of mankind's fall. Genesis 3 is also the story of the beginning of the plan of redemption. While talking to Satan about the consequences of his actions, God gives the first indicator of a coming Messiah, the One who would deliver mankind from the clutches of sin and evil.

Genesis 3:15 NIV

> *And I will put enmity (hatred, hostility) between you and the woman, and between your offspring and hers; **he will crush your head**, and you will strike his heel. (Parenthesis mine)*

Notice that the coming Messiah would be born from the offspring or seed of a **woman**. Genealogy and lineage were always traced from the man, so why was the Messiah prophesied to be born as the seed of a woman? Answer: Because this foretells the virgin birth...no man involved! Keep this in mind, it will come up in the next chapter.

The phrase "you will strike his heel" is talking about what Satan will do to Jesus on the cross. The phrase "he will crush your head" is referring to what the Messiah would do to Satan at the cross and resurrection. If I shot you in the heel, it hurts, but it's comparatively superficial and temporary. If I shot you in the head, it's fatal. Satan would have his moment, but Jesus would have the eternal crushing blow to the kingdom of darkness.

After mankind's fall into sin, God implemented His preexisting plan (1 Peter 1:20 – "God chose him as your ransom long before the world began." NLT) to rescue mankind and all of creation. This plan will find its final and ultimate manifestation when Satan is forever banished and thrown into the lake of fire.

Revelation 20:10

> *And the devil who deceived them was thrown into the lake of fire and brimstone, where the beast and the false prophet are also; and they will be tormented day and night forever and ever.*

But the plan was implemented in a major and significant way when Jesus came and fulfilled His earthly mission. The difference between the state of God's plan we are currently in versus the state of the ultimate fulfillment of that plan, is the subject of the next chapter.

Chapter 12

2

Because of 'Already but Not Yet'

Although related to the previous chapter (BECAUSE WE'RE LIVING IN A FALLEN WORLD), this reason for mankind's suffering is somewhat different. Here we're talking about suffering during the unique, transitional period of time we're presently living in, which is from the time of Jesus' earthly ministry until the final state of heaven.

The gist of 'already but not yet' theology states that when Jesus came, the Kingdom of God broke through into the world to redeem mankind from the consequences of the fall. But the fullness and absolute completion of that redemption won't be "realized" until we get to heaven. So it's ALREADY broken into the present, but it's NOT YET manifested in totality.

Already

All through the Old Testament, the Lord inspired His prophets to foretell of the coming Messiah. And then He came the moment God had appointed in His plan.

Galatians 4:4-5

> *But when the fullness of the time came (when the set time had fully come – NIV), God sent forth His Son, born of a woman, born under the Law, so that He might redeem those who were under the Law.*

Shortly after Jesus was born, His parents took Him to the temple in Jerusalem to dedicate Him. The Lord had revealed to a man in Jerusalem by the name of Simeon, that he would not die until he had seen the coming of the Messiah. It says the Holy Spirit led Simeon to the temple on the very same day that Joseph and Mary brought the small child, Jesus, into the temple. And this is what happened:

Luke 2:28-32

> He (Simeon) took Him (Jesus) into his arms, and blessed God, and said, "Now Lord, You are releasing Your bond-servant to depart in peace, according to Your word; for my eyes have seen Your salvation, which You have prepared in the presence of all peoples, **a Light of revelation** to the Gentiles, and the glory of Your people Israel."

Even before Jesus had accomplished one thing, it was known in heaven, earth and in the spirit world, that the Messiah, a Light of revelation (for He revealed the Father), had broken into darkness.

John 1:4-5,9

> In Him was life, and the life was the Light of men. The Light shines in the darkness, and the darkness did not comprehend it. ... There was the true Light which, coming into the world, enlightens every man.

This was the in-breaking of God's kingdom through the Messiah. When Jesus began His public ministry, the first words out of His mouth were about the kingdom.

Matthew 4:17

> Repent, for the kingdom of heaven is at hand.

This was the beginning of the reign of the Kingdom of God on the earth. Jesus' mission was to undo what the devil had caused at the time of the fall.

1 John 3:8

> *The Son of God appeared for this purpose,* **to destroy the works of the devil.**

And so, Jesus began to do just that. He healed, He raised the dead, He blessed, He released people from demonic possession and oppression, He gave people the Good News of the Kingdom, He set people free. Jesus proclaimed His mission in Luke 4.

Luke 4:14-21

14 *And Jesus returned to Galilee in the power of the Spirit, and news about Him spread through all the surrounding district.*

15 *And He began teaching in their synagogues and was praised by all.*

16 *And He came to Nazareth, where He had been brought up; and as was His custom, He entered the synagogue on the Sabbath, and stood up to read.*

17 *And the book of the prophet Isaiah was handed to Him. And He opened the book and found the place where it was written,*

18 *"The Spirit of the Lord is upon Me, because He anointed Me to preach the gospel to the poor. He has sent Me to proclaim release to the captives, and recovery of sight to the blind, to set free those who are oppressed,*

19 *to proclaim the favorable year of the Lord."*

20 *And He closed the book, gave it back to the attendant and sat down; and the eyes of all in the synagogue were fixed on Him.*

21 *And He began to say to them, "Today this Scripture has been fulfilled in your hearing."*

The reign of the Kingdom of God began. But wait, Adam and Eve had been given legal power of attorney to make decisions and enforce things on the earth. This authority was forfeited over to Satan after they sinned. What right did Jesus have to do anything on earth? Answer: Jesus, because He was born from a woman, a virgin, did not have the stain of sin passed on through man. Remember Romans 5:12.

Romans 5:12

> *Therefore, just as through **one man** sin entered into the world, and death through sin, and so death **spread to all men**.*

Jesus was not born through a man, and His mother was only the incubator that carried Him. If Jesus had been born through the seed of a man, He would have been no different from you and me, born into the slave market of sin. Slaves can't free slaves, only a free man can free a slave, and Jesus was that free man! So Jesus, being fully man unstained from sin, and fully God, began to overpower the devil and set people free, even before His resurrection.

Then, the cross and resurrection went a step further and totally defeated the devil, and stripped away from him all authority.

Colossians 2:13-15

> *Having forgiven us all our transgressions, having canceled out the certificate of debt consisting of decrees against us, which was hostile to us; and He has taken it out of the way, having nailed it to the cross. **When He had disarmed the rulers and authorities**, He made a public display of them, having triumphed over them through Him.*

Notice, "When He had disarmed the rulers and authorities." The powers of darkness have now been disarmed.

Hebrews 2:14

> *That through death He **might render powerless** him who had the power of death, that is, the devil.*

The devil has been disarmed and rendered powerless. He and his evil spirits no longer have legal power of attorney. They no longer have authority. Jesus legally and forcefully stripped it away from them. Notice what Jesus said after His resurrection.

Matthew 28:1

> *All authority has been given to Me in heaven and on earth.*

Revelation 1:17-18

*When I (the Apostle John) saw Him, I fell at His feet like a dead man. And He placed His right hand on me, saying, "Do not be afraid; I am the first and the last, and the living One; and I was dead, and behold, I am alive forevermore, and I have **the keys** of death and of Hades.*

Keys, in scripture, always represent authority to reign. And what did Jesus do with the keys of authority?

Matthew 16:19

*I will give you **the keys** of the kingdom of heaven; and whatever you bind on earth shall have been bound in heaven, and whatever you loose on earth shall have been loosed in heaven.*

Jesus gave the keys of authority back to mankind. And now, in this present time, we have authority to do the works of Jesus Christ.

Luke 9:1-2

*And He called the twelve together (and by extension, the Church, the Body of Christ), and **gave them power and authority** over all the demons and to heal diseases. And He sent them out to **proclaim the kingdom of God** and to perform healing.*

Notice the connection between this delegated authority to heal, and the proclamation of the kingdom of God. We're living in a time when the kingdom of God has come and is releasing people from the effects of darkness, from "the works of the devil" (1 John 3:8). It's now the Holy Spirit through the Church, followers of Jesus Christ, who are bringing into the earth this new kingdom.

It is the Holy Spirit through His church praying and acting, that the Kingdom of God becomes visible here on earth.

Matthew 6:10

Your kingdom come. Your will be done, on earth as it is in heaven.

And so, this is our commission, to be agents of introducing people to this new Kingdom, and being used of God to set people free from the dominion of darkness. Part of this is healing.

James 5:14,15

> *Is anyone among you sick? Then he must call for the elders of the church and they are to pray over him, anointing him with oil in the name of the Lord; and the prayer offered in faith will restore the one who is sick, and the Lord will raise him up, and if he has committed sins, they will be forgiven him.*

The point here—the Kingdom of God through Christ has broken into history to set people free from the suffering previously imposed by Satan. But simple observation introduces a conundrum that not everyone seems to be free.

But Not Yet

Yet, not everyone is healed or set free from this suffering. What gives?

Even though I believe it's God's will that healing, provision, long life, and all other blessings afforded us in Christ are for all who come to Him in faith seeking such blessings, not all of us experience them, even when we pray for them.

Part of this lies in understanding this transitional period we're presently in, "already but not yet." When we say "but not yet", we mean not FULLY or ABSOLUTELY yet, not in its entirety. This is true in several realms.

For example, salvation. Jesus brought salvation to the world through His substitutionary death on the cross and resurrection. It is now available to those who will accept that gift. The time to receive salvation is now, and can be experienced now.

2 Corinthians 6:2

> *Behold, now is "the acceptable time," behold, now is "the day of salvation"*

When someone makes the decision to become a Christ follower, they become "saved."

Romans 10:9

> *That if you confess with your mouth Jesus as Lord, and believe in your heart that God raised Him from the dead, you will be saved.*

Saved when? Answer: When you confess with your mouth and believe in your heart that God raised Jesus from the dead and that He is Lord. Salvation has come. Salvation is now. Yet we see this equal and parallel truth…that salvation will come in the future.

Revelation 12:10

> **Now** *the salvation, and the power, and the kingdom of our God and the authority of His Christ have come, for the accuser of our brethren has been thrown down.*

After Satan is totally defeated and is no more, it says "Now the salvation, and the power, and the kingdom of our God and the authority of His Christ have come." Whoa, I thought salvation came with Jesus at the resurrection to be experienced now! It did, but we don't experience total and absolute salvation in all its glorious fullness until heaven. So, salvation is "already but not yet."

An example of this is death. Jesus conquered death.

2 Timothy 1:10

> *Our Savior Christ Jesus,* **who abolished death** *and brought life and immortality to light through the gospel.*

Hebrews 2:14

> *Therefore, since the children share in flesh and blood, He Himself likewise also partook of the same, that through death* **He might render powerless him who had the power of death, that is, the devil.**

So death has been abolished and the one who had the power of death, the devil, has been rendered powerless.

And yet, loved ones and friends die. We all will die barring the second coming of Christ. It doesn't seem death has been conquered.

1 Corinthians 15:26

*For He must reign until He has put all His enemies under His feet. **The last enemy that will be abolished is death.***

What? Jesus Christ abolished death, but death is the last enemy that will be put under His feet? How does one explain this? The answer lies in understanding the time we're living in, a time of 'already but not yet.'

Yet another example is that, in Christ, we're free from sin and have become new creations.

2 Corinthians 5:17

Therefore if anyone is in Christ, he is a new creature; the old things passed away; behold, new things have come.

If you've accepted Jesus Christ, you're a brand new creature and that old, sinful nature is gone!

Romans 6:22 NIV

But now that you have been set free from sin and have become slaves of God, the benefit you reap leads to holiness, and the result is eternal life.

We're brand new people, old things have passed away, we've been set free from sin and now serve God and walk in holiness. Yippee! Uh oh, wait, but we still gravitate toward sin and in fact, do sin, and sometimes downright enjoy sinning! What's that about?

I'll tell what that's about, it's called "already but not yet." In other words, the full and absolute realization and experience of that freedom from sin will be in heaven. We experience it to a degree already, but it's fullest realization will be in heaven. We're new creations in Christ, but we don't experience that fully just yet.

1 John 3:2

*Beloved, now we are children of God, and it has not appeared **as yet** what we will be.*

Here is another example. We know that God has given mankind authority. As we've said before, God intended mankind to be under-rulers here on earth.

Psalm 8:6-8

> *What is man that You take thought of him, and the son of man that You care for him? Yet **You have made him a little lower than God**, and You crown him with glory and majesty! **You make him to rule over the works of Your hands; You have put all things under his feet.***

God has given back to mankind authority, yet ... our experience shows that not everything seems to act like it's under our authority. Watch the same passage from Psalm 8 quoted in the New Testament in Hebrews 2.

Hebrews 2:6-8

> *"What is man, that You remember him? Or the son of man, that You are concerned about him? "You have made him for a little while lower than the angels; You have crowned him with glory and honor, and have appointed him over the works of Your hands; You have put all things in subjection under his feet." For in subjecting all things to him, He left nothing that is not subject to him. **But now we do not yet see all things subjected to him.***

The last sentence is the kicker, "But now we do not YET see all things subjected to him." Friends, that's just reality.

We are in a transitional period right now (the church age, the age of grace), when we are living as redeemed people but we don't experience that redemption fully and absolutely without some evidence of a fallen world. Notice what Jesus said:

John 18:36

> *My kingdom is not of this world.*

His kingdom broke into this world, but it's not of this world. The absolute fullness of His kingdom is yet to come. Now we're still living in this world, so it's a transitional period we're in.

This does NOT mean that it's God will for His people to experience sickness and tragedy, but it helps us to understand a simple truth ... we're not in heaven yet.

Chapter 13

3

Because It's a Direct Attack from Satan

All sickness, pain and tragedy come either indirectly (because of the Genesis 3 fall) or directly (direct personal attack) from the devil.

Indirectly

Indirectly, we can attribute everything that robs people of life, health, provision and joy to the devil.

John 10:10

> *The thief comes only to steal and kill and destroy; I came that they may have life, and have it abundantly.*

Things that steal, kill and destroy are not from God, but from the enemy.[28] Before the fall, there was no death, sickness, disease, premature death, poverty or lack, calamity or tragedy. Satan brought all those horrible things into the earth because of mankind's sin. When Satan is finally banished forever in the lake of fire, suffering of every kind will cease.

Revelation 21:4

> *And He will wipe away every tear from their eyes; and there will no longer be any death; there will no longer be any mourning, or crying, or pain; the first things have passed away.*

If these things didn't occur before Satan tempted mankind and caused his fall in the garden, and they won't occur anymore after he is thrown into the lake of fire forever, it should be obvious where death, mourning, crying and pain come from—from Satan, not God.

All suffering comes indirectly from the devil.

Acts 10:38

> *You know of Jesus of Nazareth, how God anointed Him with the Holy Spirit and with power, and how He went about doing good and healing all <u>who were oppressed by the devil</u>, for God was with Him.*

Notice who the culprit is, the devil. All sickness and disease inflicted upon people comes from him. We need to change our thinking on this and stop saying that "maybe this is from God to teach you something or bring good out of it." Sickness is not from God!

Directly

Again, all sickness is oppression indirectly caused by the devil or by not taking care of ourselves, but some sickness, pain, tragedy and suffering come as a direct, one-on-one personal attack from the devil or an evil spirit.

Luke 13:11,16

> *And there was a woman who for eighteen years had had a sickness **caused by a spirit** (NIV - **crippled by an evil spirit**) and she was bent double, and could not straighten up at all. ... (Jesus confronting the synagogue official who was angry that Jesus was healing on the Sabbath) "Then should not this woman, a daughter of Abraham, **whom Satan has kept bound** for eighteen long years, be set free on the Sabbath day from what bound her?"*

This physical infirmity was not caused indirectly from Satan because of mankind's fall. This was a result of a direct personal attack.

Let me give you an analogy. Suppose you are suffering a financial setback because the large company you work for has experienced a major downturn and has cut salaries and eliminated bonuses for everyone. That's one thing. But now let's suppose that you found out that the CFO (Chief Financial Officer) of the company has uniquely singled you out and has been stealing from your weekly paycheck. That's quite another thing. One was a general thing that affected everybody, but this was personal!

In some cases, sickness is caused by a direct attack from an evil spirit.

Matthew 9:32,33

*As they were going out, a mute, **demon-possessed man** was brought to Him. **After the demon was cast out**, the mute man spoke; and the crowds were amazed, and were saying, "Nothing like this has ever been seen in Israel."*

Matthew 12:22,23

*Then a **demon-possessed man** who was blind and mute was brought to Jesus, and He healed him, so that the mute man spoke and saw. All the crowds were amazed, and were saying, "This man cannot be the Son of David, can he?"*

Some, not all, sickness or infirmities are caused by a direct attack of Satan or an evil spirit. The answer is obvious—the evil spirit must be cast out. And that is what believers are commanded to do IF they discern this to be the case.

Matthew 10:1

Jesus summoned His twelve disciples and gave them authority over unclean spirits, to cast them out, and to heal every kind of disease and every kind of sickness.

I would caution people from poo-pooing the reality of this cause of human suffering. Satan is real. Evil spirits are real. Some people experiencing physical or mental illness, or continual harassment in life in one area or another, are being directly oppressed by the powers of darkness. There is good news...Jesus came into this world to set people free.

1 John 3:8

The Son of God appeared for this purpose, to destroy the works of the devil.

John 8:36

So if the Son makes you free, you will be free indeed.

Conclusion—we have authority and power over Satan and evil spirits! And there are times we need to rise up in a holy, righteous anger and cast them out.

Acts 16:16-18

It happened that as we were going to the place of prayer, a slave-girl having a spirit of divination met us, who was bringing her masters much profit by fortune-telling. Following after Paul and us, she kept crying out, saying, "These men are bond-servants of the Most High God, who are proclaiming to you the way of salvation." She continued doing this for many days. But Paul was greatly annoyed, and turned and said to the spirit, "I command you in the name of Jesus Christ to come out of her!" And it came out at that very moment.

Mark 6:12-13

They went out and preached that men should repent. And they were casting out many demons and were anointing with oil many sick people and healing them.

There is a category of suffering that won't respond to medication, but will respond to a decisive action of rebuking and casting out an evil spirit that is tormenting the person. This will seem ridiculous to many people, but I can assure you based on personal experience with this type of thing, it is very real.

CHAPTER 14

4

Because We're Actively Living in Sin

One cause of suffering is due to intentionally and actively living in sin. As we saw with Adam and Eve, sin has consequences. Sin always produces bad results. That was true in the very beginning, and it's true today.

There's a difference between "sinning" (which we all do) and "living in sin", meaning we have chosen to practice sin repetitively, to sin continually as a lifestyle without repentance.

1 John 3:9

> *No one who is born of God **practices** sin, because His seed abides in him; and he cannot sin, because he is born of God. By this the children of God and the children of the devil are obvious: anyone who does not **practice** righteousness is not of God, nor the one who does not love his brother.*

The emphasis here is the *practice* of sin. All of us sin, probably daily, but some people deliberately and intentionally engage in the practice of sin. They persist in a specific sin continually. It has become a lifestyle. But intentionally living in sin opens the door to negative consequences.

The New Testament uses three main words for sin, and they all have different meanings.

1. **Paraptoma** – a blunder, an unintentional slipping into sin.

2. **Agnoema** – a sin of ignorance, wasn't aware it was a sin in the first place.

3. **Harmartia** – a willful, known sin, entered into it eyes wide open.

It is this third category of sin that we are focusing on in this chapter because it is continual, premeditated, and intentional.

Hebrews 10:26-27

*For if **we go on sinning willfully** after receiving the knowledge of the truth, there no longer remains a sacrifice for sins, but a terrifying expectation of judgment and the fury of a fire which will consume the adversaries.*

"If we go on" – means continual, unbroken by repentance. "Sinning willfully" – means premeditated, intentional, willful.

When we intentionally "thumb our nose" at God by living in violation of His commandments, we open up our lives to the consequences of sin. This is a God-instituted law of sowing and reaping.

Galatians 6:7

***Do not be deceived**, God is not mocked; for whatever a man sows, this he will also reap.*

There is a law called "sowing and reaping." It is both a natural and spiritual law. This law doesn't much care about intention, it works regardless. And notice that it says "Do not be deceived." I believe the reason the Holy Spirit inserted this little phrase is because humans tend to be deceived about this law of sowing and reaping, typically with thoughts like, "Yeah, but it won't happen to me."

We think we can bypass this law, but scripture plainly tells us not to be deceived about this…consequences will happen.

Numbers 32:23

*Behold, you have sinned against the Lord, **and be sure** your sin will find you out.*

"And be sure" – "Do not be deceived". In other words, this is a spiritual law so don't think it can be ignored. God has ordained from the beginning that if we align our lives with Him and His will, we'll experience blessings. If we intentionally go crosswise to His will, we suffer evil consequences. Deuteronomy 28 shows both the blessings of following God and the curses of going against Him.

Deuteronomy 28:1-2

> Now it shall be, if you diligently obey the Lord your God, being careful to do all His commandments which I command you today, the Lord your God will set you high above all the nations of the earth. **All these blessings** will come upon you and overtake you if you obey the Lord your God.

And then it lists all the wonderful blessings we can have as we walk with God and put Him first in our lives.

- Blessed wherever you go (3,6).
- Offspring of your body, children, will be blessed (4).
- Your animals and agriculture will be blessed (4).
- Your enemies will be defeated (7).
- You will succeed in all your endeavors (8).
- You will abound in prosperity (11,12).
- You'll experience favor in the social realm (13).

But conversely, starting in Verse 15, when we choose to disobey God, there are consequences.

Deuteronomy 28:15

> But it shall come about, if you do not obey the Lord your God, to observe to do all His commandments and His statutes with which I charge you today, that **all these curses** will come upon you and overtake you.

The verses following detail all the evil consequences that are part of the curse of sin. Here's a partial list.

- Cursed wherever you go (16).
- Offspring of your body, children, cursed (18).
- Your animals and agricultural efforts cursed (18,30,31).
- Confusion (20).
- Pestilence (21).
- Sickness (22,27,35,59,61).

- Lack of rain (23,24).
- Enemies will defeat you (25,26,49).
- Madness (28,34).
- Robbed continually (29).
- Rape (30).
- Lose your family (32,41).
- Slavery (36).
- Hunger, thirst (38,39,48).
- Social outcasts (44).
- Hostility & discord among you (54-56).

This is all part of the curse that exploded into the earth because of sin.

We need to know that when God gives commandments, it's not to rain on our parade or stifle our fun, it's because He knows best what is good for us. His commandments are always for our own protection and welfare.

Deuteronomy 6:24

*So the Lord commanded us to observe all these statutes, to fear the Lord our God **for our good always** and for our survival, as it is today.*

Deuteronomy 10:12,13

*Now, Israel, what does the Lord your God require from you, but to fear the Lord your God, to walk in all His ways and love Him, and to serve the Lord your God with all your heart and with all your soul, and to keep the Lord's commandments and His statutes which I am commanding you today **for your good**?*

A parent is wiser than a four-year-old child. When a parent tells a four-year-old not to play with matches, it's for the child's own good. But we must start with the basic presupposition that the parent is wiser than the child. The same thing applies to God and His children. We must embrace the fact that God is wiser than you and me, and should trust that His commandments are for our own good.

There is a natural and a spiritual component to this point. In the natural, for example, if one sleeps around with multiple partners, there's a good chance they will contract a sexually transmitted disease. It's called sowing and reaping.

If a person cheats on their taxes, there's a good chance the IRS will discover that and impose a hefty fine, or worse, prison.

If a person commits and continues in an adulterous affair, chances are that will be discovered and result in broken families and ruined lives.

A person who continues looking at pornography will eventually experience evil consequences. *Wired for Intimacy: How Pornography Hijacks the Male Brain*, by William M. Struthers, documents the negative effects of pornography by rewiring the neuro-pathways in the brain. It's called sowing and reaping.[29]

Just as we saw with the natural, so there is a spiritual side to this point as well. Remember what we said earlier in chapter 5, that when Adam and Eve sinned, the curse exploded into the earth. That "curse storm" hit humanity in the form of sickness, disease, poverty and lack, premature death, disabilities, all forms of mental illness and oppression. The storm is out there.

But God blesses those who walk before Him in obedience.

Isaiah 1:19a NIV

If you are willing and obedient, you will eat the good things of the land.

But when we actively choose to live in sin, the umbrella of divine blessing and protection folds or shrinks up and the storm of the curse gets in.

Isaiah 1:19b NIV

But if you resist and rebel, you will be devoured by the sword.

The law of sowing and reaping works both ways, positive and negative.

When we connect and walk with God through His Son, Jesus Christ, and while:
- choosing to not intentionally live in (practice) sin (this chapter, Chapter 14), and
- walking in His known will for our lives (Chapter 15), and
- believing/trusting God for His promises of protection, healing, provision, guidance and wisdom (Chapter 16),

we can live with God's blessings with Him being our refuge, protection and deliverance from the *curse storm* mentioned earlier.

At the risk of seeming overly simplistic, it's like we're living with the umbrella of God's blessings that, to a great degree, shelters us from the full measure of the curse.

To be clear, the storm touches all of us at one time or another, simply because we're living in a fallen world. Even with an umbrella, some rain gets in, depending on the severity of the storm. The umbrella is not a bubble that prevents all rain, but it does shelter us from the full impact and force of the storm brought on by the curse.

Some will argue that Christians can't expect God's protection from the *curse storm* that brings sickness, disease, premature death, tragedy, calamity, poverty and lack, and mental and emotional oppression. But I would disagree. Although none of us will experience the fullest degree or measure of this protection from the curse in this life (note the other chapters here in Part 3), we can expect a great deal of protection from God in these areas.

Galatians 3:13

> *Christ redeemed us from the curse of the Law*, *having become a curse for us—for it is written, "Cursed is everyone who hangs on a tree"*

We are redeemed from the curse, not just the curse of eternal damnation due to our sin, but from other forms of the curse (refer to Deuteronomy 28:15ff).

If we will walk with God through Jesus Christ, stay in His will, say no to sin, and actively trust Him for His promises and blessings, we can expect those promises and blessings to be *realized* in our lives.

Psalm 91 NIV

1 *Whoever dwells in the shelter of the Most High will rest in the shadow of the Almighty.*

2 *I will say of the Lord, "He is my refuge and my fortress, my God, in whom I trust."*

3 *Surely he will save you from the fowler's snare and from the deadly pestilence.*

4 *He will cover you with his feathers, and under his wings you will find refuge; his faithfulness will be your shield and rampart.*

5 *You will not fear the terror of night, nor the arrow that flies by day,*

6 *nor the pestilence that stalks in the darkness, nor the plague that destroys at midday.*

7 *A thousand may fall at your side, ten thousand at your right hand, but it will not come near you.*

8 *You will only observe with your eyes and see the punishment of the wicked.*

9 *If you say, "The Lord is my refuge," and you make the Most High your dwelling,*

10 *no harm will overtake you, no disaster will come near your tent.*

> 11 *For he will command his angels concerning you to guard you in all your ways;*
>
> 12 *they will lift you up in their hands, so that you will not strike your foot against a stone.*
>
> 13 *You will tread on the lion and the cobra; you will trample the great lion and the serpent.*
>
> 14 *"Because he loves me," says the Lord, "I will rescue him; I will protect him, for he acknowledges my name.*
>
> 15 *He will call on me, and I will answer him; I will be with him in trouble, I will deliver him and honor him.*
>
> 16 *With long life I will satisfy him and show him my salvation."*

What I'm NOT saying is that trouble won't come. Verse 15, "I will be with him in trouble," shows trouble comes. But we can overcome and experience God's protection and victory in times of trouble.

The flip side of the coin is when we intentionally live in sin, sin that is unrepented of. In that case, our prayers or cry for help are hindered.

Psalm 66:18

> *If I regard wickedness in my heart, the Lord will not hear.*

Isaiah 59:1-2

> *Behold, the Lord's hand is not so short that it cannot save; nor is His ear so dull that it cannot hear. But your iniquities have made a separation between you and your God, and your sins have hidden His face from you so that He does not hear.*

"Hyper-Grace"[30] advocates will charge that these Old Testament scriptures aren't relevant to those of us living in the New Testament era. Really? What about what the Apostle Peter said in his first letter?

1 Peter 3:7

> *You husbands in the same way, live with your wives in an understanding way, as with someone weaker, since she is a*

woman; and show her honor as a fellow heir of the grace of life, **so that your prayers will not be hindered.**

A husband's prayers can be hindered if he's mistreating his wife (that's called sin).

The idea of God's blessings being blocked or hindered by a person living in sin is not applicable to those of us living in the New Testament era? Someone should have informed Jesus about that.

John 5 is the story of the lame man by the pool of Bethsaida, whom Jesus healed. Afterwards, the now healed man found Jesus in the temple, and Jesus said something to him that is quite interesting.

John 5:14

Afterward Jesus found him in the temple and said to him, 'Behold, you have become well; **do not sin anymore, so that nothing worse happens to you.'**

However you cut it, there evidently is a connection between sin and bad things happening as a result. Intentionally living in sin creates some holes in the umbrella of protection.

The "practice of sin" (1 John 3:9) will result in a measure of the curse getting in. Is this God's judgment? No, it's related to this spiritual law of sowing and reaping, a law we are told that we should NOT be deceived about. One can't be intentionally living in sin and "dwelling the shelter of the Most High" at the same time!

This does NOT apply to those walking with God to the best of their ability, and who are endeavoring to obey Him, walking in His will and trusting Him for the fulfillment of His promises.

When people willfully live in sin and bad things happen as a result, some people will say it's God causing them to suffer, but that's not the case. Yes, it's God who created this law of sowing and reaping, so one could say that God is responsible in an indirect sense. But what is really happening here is the spiritual (and natural) law of sowing and reaping.

God, on occasion, even in the New Testament, has executed judgment upon wickedness (e.g. - Ananias and Sapphira in Acts 5:1-11; Herod in Acts 12:23; the man continuing in sexual immorality without repentance in 1 Corinthians 5:5; Jezebel and her followers in Revelation 3:22,23; not correctly discerning the Lord's body in the Lord's supper, 1 Corinthians 11:27-30). But don't take this as the norm. Yet, people think that God delights in that. They are wrong.

Lamentations 3:33 NLT

For he does not enjoy hurting people or causing them sorrow.

Many people have a warped image of God, believing that He wants and even enjoys judgment upon the wicked. This is not true. In any legitimate judicial system there has to be punishment for the transgressor. That is part and parcel of a fair system of jurisprudence. But "the Judge of all the earth" (Genesis 18:25) doesn't delight in doing so.

Ezekiel 18:5, 9, 20-32

5 *But if a man is righteous and practices justice and righteousness, ...*

9 *if he walks in My statutes and My ordinances so as to deal faithfully—he is righteous and will surely live," declares the Lord God.*

20 *The person who sins will die (umbrella with holes in it). The son will not bear the punishment for the father's iniquity, nor will the father bear the punishment for the son's*

iniquity; the righteousness of the righteous will be upon himself, and the wickedness of the wicked will be upon himself.

21 *"But if the wicked man turns from all his sins which he has committed and observes all My statutes and practices justice and righteousness, he shall surely live (umbrella with no holes); he shall not die.*

22 *All his transgressions which he has committed will not be remembered against him; because of his righteousness which he has practiced, he will live.*

23 **Do I have any pleasure in the death of the wicked," declares the Lord God, "rather than that he should turn from his ways and live?**

24 *"But when a righteous man turns away from his righteousness, commits iniquity and does according to all the abominations that a wicked man does, will he live? All his righteous deeds which he has done will not be remembered for his treachery which he has committed and his sin which he has committed; for them he will die (umbrella with holes, the curse gets in).*

25 *Yet you say, 'The way of the Lord is not right.' Hear now, O house of Israel!* **Is My way not right? Is it not your ways that are not right?** *(in other words—don't pin it on Me!)*

26 *When a righteous man turns away from his righteousness, commits iniquity and dies because of it, for his iniquity which he has committed he will die.*

27 *Again, when a wicked man turns away from his wickedness which he has committed and practices justice and righteousness, he will save his life.*

28 *Because he considered and turned away from all his transgressions which he had committed, he shall surely live; he shall not die.*

29 *But the house of Israel says, 'The way of the Lord is not right.'* **Are My ways not right, O house of Israel? Is it not your ways that are not right?**

> 30 *"Therefore I will judge you, O house of Israel, each according to his conduct," declares the Lord God. "Repent and turn away from all your transgressions, so that iniquity may not become a stumbling block to you.*
>
> 31 *Cast away from you all your transgressions which you have committed and make yourselves a new heart and a new spirit!* **For why will you die, O house of Israel?**
>
> 32 **For I have no pleasure in the death of anyone who dies,"** *declares the Lord God. "***Therefore, repent and live.***"*

Verse 29 - But the house of Israel says, 'The way of the Lord is not right.'

Isn't this typical humanity? It shows that punished people get mad at the legislators (who created the laws) and the judge (who declared a verdict and the issued an appropriate sentence). In this case, God is both Legislator and Judge. But God doesn't delight in punishment that results from the law of sowing and reaping or even from His system of jurisprudence, where punishment must be meted out. He wants people to repent, live and come under His blessings.

The norm for God's reaction to our continued sin is a longing for us to return to Him, so that grace and forgiveness may be given and received. He is the father in the parable of the prodigal son (Luke 15:11-32) who expresses deep joy upon a returning child who repents.

Isaiah 30:18 NLT

> *So the LORD must wait for you to come to him so he can show you his love and compassion.*

If sin produces suffering, it is caused by this law of sowing and reaping.

Remember we talked about three kinds of sin: *paraptomas* (blundering or slipping into sin), *agnoemas* (sins of ignorance), and *harmartias* (willful, known, intentional sins). Here is the wonderful good news of Jesus Christ:

1 John 1:9

> *If we confess our* **sins***, He is faithful and righteous to forgive us our* **sins** *and to cleanse us from* **all unrighteousness***.*

"Sins" here is *harmartia*. The verse is saying this: If we confess our *harmartias* (willful, known sins), He is faithful and just to forgive us of those *harmartias*, but not only that, He'll also cleanse us from ALL unrighteousness, including all the *paraptomas* and *agnoemas*.

In concluding this chapter, I need to make an important point. Although I stand by the arguments made in this chapter, I must also stress that we must guard ourselves from automatically connecting suffering with the idea of living in intentional sin. Keep in mind this is only one of ten reasons for suffering and it is geared toward those who intentionally thumb their nose at God and live in sin.

To assume suffering or tragedy is the cause of sin is to make the same mistake people made when talking to Jesus in Luke 13.

Luke 13:1-5

> *Now on the same occasion there were some present who reported to Him about the Galileans whose blood Pilate had mixed with their sacrifices. And Jesus said to them, "**Do you suppose that these Galileans were greater sinners than all other Galileans because they suffered this fate?** I tell you, no, but unless you repent, you will all likewise perish. **Or do you suppose that those eighteen on whom the tower in Siloam fell and killed them were worse culprits than all the men who live in Jerusalem?** I tell you, no, but unless you repent, you will all likewise perish."*

In response to some people bringing this up to Jesus, He mentioned two tragedies here and then asked the question (in my words), "Do you think these happened because of their sin was greater than anyone else's? No way!" Here Jesus disconnects the idea that their suffering was caused by their sin.

We need to guard ourselves from the charge that their suffering was the result of their sin. This was the accusation of Job's friends (Chapter 9), and the Lord rebuked them for their error (Job 42:7ff).

We must also remember that Jesus suffered FOR our sins already.

1 Peter 3:18

For Christ also died FOR sins once for all, the just FOR the unjust, so that He might bring us to God.

Jesus already paid the penalty for our sins. If a person's suffering is connected to their deliberate living in sin, it is more a case of the immutable law of sowing and reaping, rather than the direct judgment of God.

And keep in mind what God's heart is—He has no pleasure in the death of the wicked, and His desire is that they turn from their sin and live in His blessings (Ezekiel 18:23).

CHAPTER 15

5

Because We're Living Outside of God's Will

Although this is related to the previous chapter (BECAUSE WE'RE ACTIVELY LIVING IN SIN), it is a little different in that it is a specific kind of straying from God, one of knowing God's will for one's life but purposely ignoring it. But it has the same effect due to the law of sowing and reaping.

When we know God's will for our lives but purposely ignore or go against it, we are in disobedience to the known will of God and will suffer consequences for that disobedience. Sometimes it's simply the law of sowing and reaping, and in other cases it is God taking an action to move us back into His will. The classic story that comes to mind is Jonah.

Jonah 1:1-3

> *The word of the Lord came to Jonah the son of Amittai saying, "Arise, go to Nineveh the great city and cry against it, for their wickedness has come up before Me." But Jonah rose up to flee to Tarshish from the presence of the Lord.*

God had a plan for Jonah. God wanted Jonah to go to Nineveh and preach to them a message of God's reality and the need to repent of their wickedness. Jonah declined and ran away from the assignment. One reason was because the people of Nineveh were not Jews and he was afraid of their reaction to his preaching.

If you're familiar with the story, you know what happened next—Jonah gets swallowed by a big fish, probably a whale. He was in the whale for three days and three nights. I've never been in a whale's stomach for three days and nights, but I believe I'm on safe ground here to say that Jonah suffered during this time.

This suffering was caused by Jonah knowing God's will, but intentionally running away from it. When we go against the will of God for our lives, life can get rough.

I heard the story of a man who was rubbing and petting his cat the wrong way or direction. The cat kept getting annoyed by this and finally hissed and growled at him, at which point the man said, "Well, dummy, just turn around!" Sometimes (certainly not always) when life is frustrating and going the wrong way, we need to turn around, because we could be out of the will of God.

I've heard stories of men and women who were called by God into the ministry, but intentionally avoided it. It always resulted in heartache and never blessing.

But let's not limit this to those called to the ministry. God calls different people to different assignments using different spiritual gifts. When we fail to use those gifts for God's glory we run the risk of the blessings of God being withdrawn from our lives. Again, most likely that is the result of the spiritual law of sowing and reaping. The Apostle Paul gave a warning about this.

1 Timothy 4:14

Do not neglect the spiritual gift within you.

The Apostle Peter talks about this as well.

1 Peter 4:10 NLT

God has given each of you a gift from his great variety of spiritual gifts. Use them well to serve one another.

It's not the purpose or scope of this book to teach about spiritual gifts, but the question needs to be asked: Do you know what your spiritual gifts are? Are you using them faithfully? If not, take the time to research the subject of spiritual gifts, take an assessment, and then get off the bench as a spectator and start using them for the kingdom of God.

If you need a place to start, I'd recommend reading Bruce Bugbee's book: What You Do Best in the Body of Christ: Discover Your Spiritual Gifts, Personal Style, and God-Given Passion (Zondervan, 2005); or S.H.A.P.E.: Finding and Fulfilling Your

Unique Purpose for Life, by Erik Rees, with Rick Warren (Zondervan, 2008).

Another biblical example of someone living outside of God's will is King Saul in 1 Samuel 13. Saul and Israel's army went out to battle with the formidable army of the Philistines. Saul was supposed to wait for the prophet Samuel to come and pray and make a sacrifice before the battle. Saul waited seven days and then grew impatient.

1 Samuel 13:9

So Saul said, "Bring to me the burnt offering and the peace offerings."

Only the prophet and priest were allowed to make an offering like that to the Lord. King Saul strayed outside his calling and intentionally operated outside of God's will. Soon the prophet Samuel came and reprimanded Saul.

1 Samuel 13:13-14

Samuel said to Saul, "You have acted foolishly; you have not kept the commandment of the Lord your God, which He commanded you, for now the Lord would have established your kingdom over Israel forever. But now your kingdom shall not endure.

Saul's reign as king suffered as a result. Ignoring God's will or operating outside of God's will have consequences.

So what's the remedy? Answer: like Jonah, repent and get back into God's will. It's never too late to do that. If you're straying outside of God's will or calling for your life, repent and get back to what you were called to do. What has God gifted you with? What are your God-given passions? Are you using them for the greater glory of God and for expressing God's love to people? Numbers 32 describes two kinds of people.

Numbers 32:11,12

*'None of the men who came up from Egypt, from twenty years old and upward, shall see the land which I swore to Abraham, to Isaac and to Jacob; **for they did not follow Me fully**, except*

> *Caleb the son of Jephunneh the Kenizzite and Joshua the son of Nun, **for they have followed the Lord fully**.'*

There are two kinds of people. Those who follow the Lord fully and those who don't. The blessings of God are for those who are willing to follow God fully, not hold back on their own terms. That doesn't mean they are perfect. It doesn't mean they don't sin or fail, but it does mean they have a sincere intention, followed by action, to follow and serve the Lord.

Deuteronomy 5:33 NIV

> *Walk in obedience to all that the Lord your God has commanded you, so that you may live and prosper and prolong your days in the land that you will possess.*

A Place Call 'There'

There is a place where God wants you to be in order for you to experience His fullest blessings. It's like a receiver in football running his planned route so he can receive the pass. There is a time and place for him to be. If he's there at that time and place, all things being equal, he receives the pass. If he's not there at that time and place, he doesn't. He "suffers" an incomplete pass.

God has a plan for all of us. He wants us to follow His known will so we can receive the pass so to speak, in other words, to receive the blessing. I like the story of Elijah from 1 Kings 17. God told Elijah to be at a certain place in order to receive and experience God's blessing of provision.

1 Kings 17:2-4

> *The word of the Lord came to him (Elijah), saying, "Go away from here and turn eastward, and hide yourself by the brook Cherith, which is east of the Jordan. It shall be that you will drink of the brook, and I have commanded the ravens to provide for you **there**."*

"I have commanded the ravens to provide for you...**there**!" There is a place called "there", and the Lord wants to provide for us...there. If we knowingly ignore God's plan for our lives, in whatever degree, we'll experience, shall we say, *less than* God's best for our lives.

Missionary Wayne Myers (based in Mexico City) put it this way:

> *I would rather be in a dugout canoe floating down the Amazon fighting off crocodiles with a toothpick, in the will of God, than driving down a Dallas freeway in a convertible out of the will of God.*

If you have been living outside of the known will of God for your life, repent and get "there" so you can fulfill God's will and calling for your life. If it's not possible, then repent and ask God to lead you to a new assignment. He is gracious and compassionate and will give you a second chance.

Blueprint or Plan?

Is God's will for us more like a blueprint or a plan? What's the difference?

A blueprint is very detailed and specific. One must not err even the slightest with a blueprint or else the whole structure can fall. A plan is more general and allows for some wiggle room. Although the principle of "a place called there" still applies, the "there" may change from time to time and be more flexible than we think.

I believe God's will for our lives is more like a plan than a blueprint. He gives us gifts, passions and a unique temperament, and guides us to use those for His glory and to bless people. And, as long as we sincerely ask God to lead us and endeavor to discern His plan, we must relax, be at peace, and trust that He is guiding us and we are living in His will.

In earlier days I always seemed to worry about God's will. I put it as such a lofty and mysterious thing that it became the fourth Person of the Godhead: Father, Son, Holy Spirit, and God's will. But it only resulted in anxiety. The Lord doesn't want us to get all uptight about His will. If we're seeking Him with a sincere heart, we can be sure He will guide us.

Proverbs 20:24 NLT

> *The Lord directs our steps, so why try to understand everything along the way?*

Those words "so why try to understand everything along the way" are basically saying, "Relax and trust Me." If, for one reason or another, we miss God's will or "a place called there," if we seek Him, He will adjust our course. This is true no matter what age or life situation.

Proverbs 3:5-6 NLT

Trust in the Lord with all your heart; do not depend on your own understanding. Seek his will in all you do, and he will show you which path to take.

The key is that we sincerely seek His will, and don't plunge headlong into endeavors that we decide all by ourselves without His guidance. We need to avoid boasting about the "I decided" track.

James 4:13-16

Come now, you who say, "Today or tomorrow we will go to such and such a city, and spend a year there and engage in business and make a profit." Yet you do not know what your life will be like tomorrow. You are just a vapor that appears for a little while and then vanishes away. Instead, **you ought to say, "If the Lord wills, we will live and also do this or that.**" *But as it is, you boast in your arrogance; all such boasting is evil.*

Sometimes suffering is the result of intentionally living outside of God's will or call for our lives. Sometimes it's because we question God's will or are afraid His will won't match up to who we are (gifts, passions, temperament). But God knows more than we do. He knows us better than we know ourselves. He is the Alpha and Omega, the beginning and the end, and will lead us into His plan...IF we allow Him.

Jeremiah 29:1

For I know the plans that I have for you,' declares the Lord, 'plans for welfare and not for calamity, to give you a future and a hope.

CHAPTER 16

6

Because We Haven't Appropriated God's Promises

Sometimes people suffer because they haven't prayed and asked God for healing, financial provision, guidance or protection.

James 4:2 NLT

You don't have what you want because you don't ask God for it.

The King James Version is succinct: "Ye have not, because ye ask not."

God's blessings of healing, financial or material provision, protection, and guidance do NOT fall upon us like ripe cherries off a tree. Most Christians think, "Well, if I just love God and play nice in the sandbox with others, God will heal, protect, and provide for me." But this is not true. If God automatically did all those things just because we went to church and were good little troopers, why would we have James 4:2 (*you have not because you ask not*)? Why would we have Matthew 7:7-11?

Matthew 7:7-11

Ask, and it will be given to you; seek, and you will find; knock, and it will be opened to you. For everyone who asks receives, and he who seeks finds, and to him who knocks it will be opened. Or what man is there among you who, when his son asks for a loaf, will give him a stone? Or if he asks for a fish, he will not give him a snake, will he? If you then, being evil, know how to

> *give good gifts to your children, how much more will your*
> *Father who is in heaven give what is good to those who ask Him!*

If we automatically received and doors were automatically opened, why would Jesus have given us this admonition?

The problem is that we "assume" God's blessings and promises. Assume means "take for granted"." So most of us just tool along in life and take for granted, or assume, that we'll stay healthy, protected and provided for. Not true. I want to show you a critical point from Romans 5.

Romans 5:1-2 NIV

> *Therefore, since we have been justified through faith, we have*
> *peace with God through our Lord Jesus Christ, through whom*
> *we **have gained access by faith into this grace** in which we*
> *now stand.*

"Have gained access by faith into this grace." That's true for salvation and it's also true for all of God's blessings that come through God's grace. "Grace," besides the classic definition of *the unmerited favor of God*, could also be described as *the sum total of all the blessings and promises that we have in Christ.*

But our access, that is to say, our doorway or entranceway (Strong's Concordance, *admission*[31]) into those blessings is our faith—praying in faith to receive and experience those blessings.

Mark 5 tells the story of a woman who had a hemorrhage for twelve years (verse 25). This lady pressed through the crowd and touched the edge of Jesus' robe. As soon as she did, she was healed. Jesus turned to her and said something important.

Mark 5:34

> *Daughter, **your faith has made you well**; go in peace and be*
> *healed of your affliction.*

Wait—isn't it more accurate to say that it was God's power that made her well? Of course it was God's healing power that made her well, but that's not what Jesus said. He said it was her faith that made her well. There's a "God part" and a "human part" to this. The woman's part was to have faith and touch Jesus. Her faith was the thing that tapped into the power of God, just like a copper wire touching an electrical source.

The woman's access into the blessing of healing provided by God's grace...was her faith! And if she hadn't taken that action, she would not have been healed.

Apprōpriãte

This brings us to an important word, "appropriate" (ap-pró-pri-āte). To experience these blessings, we are instructed in Scripture to "appropriate" these blessings by praying in faith and asking for them. "Ask and you shall receive" (John 16:24).

The word "appropriate" means "to take possession of." If you have money in the bank, it's not going to help you one bit until you take possession of it by writing a check or withdrawing that money somehow. Even though the money is yours, you still have to take an action that taps into it or takes possession of it.

Here's an example. God had promised Moses, Joshua and the Israelites the present land of Israel even before they crossed over the Jordan River to enter that land.

Joshua 21:43

*So the LORD **gave Israel all the land** he had sworn to give their ancestors, and **they took possession of it** and settled there.*

Even though God had promised the land to them, they had to go in and possess it.

Joshua 1:3

*Every place on which the sole of your foot treads, **I have given it to you** (past tense), just as I spoke to Moses.*

What God is saying here is, "Even though I've given it to you, you still have to go in and take possession of it." You have to take a step and place your feet on it. In other words, even though it was theirs legally, they had to "appropriate" the promise by walking in and taking possession if it. And what they did with their feet, we do with our faith in prayer.

James 5:15

> *And the prayer offered in faith will restore the one who is sick, and the Lord will raise him up.*

"Wait, I thought it's God's power that restores the sick." It is, but it's the prayer of faith that taps into that power. "Have gained access by faith into this grace (Romans 5:2)."

To experience God's blessings of healing, financial and material provision, divine protection and guidance, we must "appropriate" God's promises by going to Him in prayer, and receiving by faith those blessings. *You have not, because you ask not* (James 4:2).

Ephesians 2:7 talks about "the riches of His grace." We are so grateful for these riches that come to us through God's grace. But these riches and blessings don't automatically fall on us, we must pray and appropriate them by faith.

Matthew 21:22 NIV

> *If you believe, you will receive whatever you **ask** for in prayer.*

Mark 11:24 NIV

> *Whatever you **ask** for in prayer, <u>believe</u> that you have received it, and it will be yours.*

Yes, God already knows what we need before we ask Him (Matthew 6:8), but He still wants us to ask in faith in order to receive.

Earlier we quoted James 4:2, "You don't have what you want because you don't ask God for it." But, in the same book of James, it adds something else—we must ask in faith, believing.

James 1:5-8

> *Ask of God, who gives to all generously and without reproach, and it will be given to him. **But he must ask in faith without any doubting,** for the one who doubts is like the surf of the sea, driven and tossed by the wind. For that man ought not to expect that he will receive anything from the Lord, being a double-minded man, unstable in all his ways.*

"But he must ask in faith without any doubting." It's not just praying. It's not just asking. It's praying and asking in faith without any doubting.

The point of this chapter is that some suffering, not all, but some, is caused by our lack of going to God in prayer and appropriating God promises and blessings by faith.

Ephesians 6 talks about the armor of God that we are to put on, and mentions the shield of faith.

Ephesians 6:16

*In addition to all, **taking up the shield of faith** with which you will be able to extinguish all the flaming arrows of the evil one.*

The "evil one" is Satan, and he is constantly shooting arrows at us in the form of sickness, disease, poverty and lack, temptation to sin, confusion, accidents, tragedy, calamity, and all manner of suffering. But we must take up the shield of faith to extinguish those arrows.

The understood subject of the admonition is "you," YOU take up the shield of faith. If you don't do it, it won't get done.

Question: What if one DOES NOT hold up the shield of faith, what happens? Answer: Obviously, the fiery arrows of the devil will get through and the person will experience an attack.

When this happens, people will say, "Well, I guess God allowed it for a reason" or, "Well, I guess God is just testing my faith," or similar things, when all the while they didn't put up the shield of faith by praying in faith and appropriating God's promises in prayer.

James 4:7

Resist the devil and he will flee from you.

Question: What if one DOESN'T resist the devil and just lets it happen uncontested? Answer: Then the devil won't flee. Yet, we have a part to play by resisting his attacks and praying in faith to receive and walk in God's blessings.

As quoted earlier, Jesus said, "If you believe, you will receive whatever you ask for in prayer." Receiving is connected to asking in faith, believing. Therefore believing is an important determining factor on what we experience in life. Believing is the issue.

Matthew 9:27-30

*As Jesus went on from there, two blind men followed Him, crying out, "Have mercy on us, Son of David!" When He entered the house, the blind men came up to Him, and Jesus said to them, **"Do you believe that I am able to do this**?" They said to Him, "Yes, Lord." Then He touched their eyes, saying, "It shall be done to you according to your faith." And their eyes were opened.*

Jesus was probing to see where they were at, "Do you believe that I'm able to do this?" Again, believing (trust, faith), is the key here.

In Mark 9 we have an interesting story that stresses this point. The disciples brought a demon possessed boy to Jesus whom they couldn't cast out. Let's pick up what happened here because Jesus said something pivotal.

Mark 9:14-23

14 *When they (Jesus, Peter, James and John – from the Mount of Transfiguration) came back to the disciples, they saw a large crowd around them, and some scribes arguing with them.*

15 *Immediately, when the entire crowd saw Him, they were amazed and began running up to greet Him.*

16 *And He asked them, "What are you discussing with them?"*

17 *And one of the crowd answered Him, "Teacher, I brought You my son, possessed with a spirit which makes him mute;*

18 *and whenever it seizes him, it slams him to the ground and he foams at the mouth, and grinds his teeth and stiffens out. I told Your disciples to cast it out, and they could not do it."*

19 *And He answered them and said, "O unbelieving generation, how long shall I be with you? How long shall I put up with you? Bring him to Me!"*

20 *They brought the boy to Him. When he saw Him, immediately the spirit threw him into a convulsion, and falling to the ground, he began rolling around and foaming at the mouth.*

21 *And He asked his father, "How long has this been happening to him?" And he said, "From childhood.*

> 22 *It has often thrown him both into the fire and into the water to destroy him. **But if You can do anything**, take pity on us and help us!"*
>
> 23 *And Jesus said to him, "'**If You can?**' All things are possible to him who believes."*

The man asked Jesus, "If You can do anything, take pity on us and help us!"

Can you imagine asking God, "If you CAN do anything, please help?" Yikes! Jesus repeated the absurdity of what he said, "If you can?"—meaning Himself, in other words, "If I can? Ha!" I believe the New Living Translation renders the question correctly, **"What do you mean, 'If I can'?"**

Jesus is basically saying to the man, "What do you mean if I can? This is not about My ability, it's about your ability to believe! Anything is possible to him who believes! If YOU can believe, that's the issue here!"

When it comes down to appropriating God's blessings by faith, we have two questions regarding God: 1) Is He able? and 2) Is He willing?

According to what we just read here in Mark 9 with the father of the demon possessed boy, and what we already read in Chapter 10 (Matthew 8:1-3) with the leper who asked Jesus if He was willing, we know two things: Jesus is both able and willing. It now becomes an issue if we will believe.

Prayer affects what happens in this world. Two great examples of this are Abraham's (Genesis 18:16ff) and Moses' (Exodus 32) intercession that stayed or prevented (at least temporarily) God's judgment to fall. Let's look at the case of Moses.

This occurred as Moses was just about to come down from Mount Sinai where he had received the tablets with the ten commandments. Before he left, the Lord pointed out to Moses that his brother and right-hand man, Aaron, and all the Israelites, had made a gold calf to worship instead of the one, true God.

Exodus 32:7-10

> 7 *Then the Lord spoke to Moses, "Go down at once, for your people, whom you brought up from the land of Egypt, have corrupted themselves.*
>
> 8 *They have quickly turned aside from the way which I commanded them. They have made for themselves a molten*

> *calf, and have worshiped it and have sacrificed to it and said, 'This is your god, O Israel, who brought you up from the land of Egypt!'"*
>
> 9 *The Lord said to Moses, "I have seen this people, and behold, they are an obstinate people.*
>
> 10 *Now then let Me alone, that My anger may burn against them and that I may destroy them; and I will make of you a great nation."*

God's plan was to destroy the whole bunch of them and begin with Moses a new, called-out people who would follow, worship and serve Him. When Moses heard what God was about to do—he interceded.

Exodus 32:11-14

> 11 *Then Moses entreated the Lord his God, and said, "O Lord, why does Your anger burn against Your people whom You have brought out from the land of Egypt with great power and with a mighty hand?*
>
> 12 *Why should the Egyptians speak, saying, 'With evil intent He brought them out to kill them in the mountains and to destroy them from the face of the earth'? Turn from Your burning anger and change Your mind about doing harm to Your people.*
>
> 13 *Remember Abraham, Isaac, and Israel, Your servants to whom You swore by Yourself, and said to them, 'I will multiply your descendants as the stars of the heavens, and all this land of which I have spoken I will give to your descendants, and they shall inherit it forever.'"*
>
> 14 *So the Lord changed His mind about the harm which He said He would do to His people.*

Psalm 106 gives us more insight.

Psalm 106:23

> *Therefore He said that He would destroy them, had not Moses His chosen one stood in the breach before Him, to turn away His wrath from destroying them.*

Prayer and intercession changed what happened here on Planet Earth.

Some people will recoil with this chapter because it places some responsibility on us to pray and ask in faith—"But he must ask in faith without any doubting" (James 1:6). We want to place all responsibility on God. But many times God would lovingly respond to us, "Dear child of mine, I have given you many promises and blessings which you are not trusting Me for. I have given you a shield of faith which you are not raising up. I have given you the name above all names, the name of Jesus, to resist the devil, which you are not speaking."

Not all suffering is caused by our failure to appropriate God's promises and blessings, but certainly some of it is.

CHAPTER 17

7

Because of Man's Inhumanity to Man

Much, if not most, of the suffering in this world is caused by man's inhumanity to man. Most likely this is the category of suffering that comes to mind when people ask, "Why doesn't God just stop all the suffering?"

It's not hard to tabulate all the examples of this. Here are just a few of the killings that have taken place down through history[32]:

- An Lushan Rebellion (China): 755-764 A.D. – 36,000,000
- Genghas Kan: 1206-1226 A.D. – 40,000,000
- Soviet famine: 1939-1945 - 7.5 million
- Cambodian genocide: 1975-1979 – 3 million
- Armenian genocide: 1915-1922 - 1.5 million
- Assyrian (Ottoman) genocide: 1915-1923 – 750,000
- Rwandan genocide: 1994 – 1 million
- Civil War: 1861-1865 – 620,000
- World War I: 1914-1918 – 17 million
- World War II: 1939-1945 – 60 million
- Vietnam War: 1954-1975 – 1.3 million

Add to this, the current suffering caused by:
- Human trafficking
- Domestic abuse
- Slavery
- Hunger/starvation (every minute 2 children die of starvation[33])
- Islamic terrorism

As I write this chapter, the untold suffering of people in Syria, Iraq, Sudan, and North Korea, serve as current proof of the point.

There was a time that philosophers tried to sell the idea that mankind is basically good. The atrocities of the 19th, 20th, and 21st centuries have been the death knell to that idea. Mankind should have listened to God on this one because He spoke to that point a long time ago.

Romans 3:10-12

*There is none righteous, not even one; there is none who understands, there is none who seeks for God; all have turned aside, together they have become useless; **there is none who does good, there is not even one**.*

Jeremiah 17:9 NLT

The human heart is the most deceitful of all things, and desperately wicked. Who really knows how bad it is?

One characteristic of humanity is, in fact, their inhumanity. The second recorded sin in the Bible was murder (Cain and Abel in Genesis 4). Envy, jealousy, and murder have been going on since that time.

There is another level of man's inhumanity to man, and that is when those with resources (money, food, clothes, shelter, protection) don't share with those without. When those repenting of their sins asked John the Baptist what they should do now that they've repented, he had a poignant answer.

Luke 3:10-11

The crowds asked, "What should we do?" John replied, "If you have two shirts, give one to the poor. If you have food, share it with those who are hungry."

While we may condemn the suffering, it's possible we share in it by our complacency and inaction.

James 4:17

Therefore, to one who knows the right thing to do and does not do it, to him it is sin.

The philosophical disconnect happens when God gets blamed for mankind's inhumanity to man. Why would people blame God for what Hitler did to the Jews? Why would He get blamed for the atrocities in Syria and Iraq?

God hates evil. God hates man's inhumanity to man and therefore He should not be blamed for it. And God wants us to hate evil as well.

Psalm 97:10

Hate evil, you who love the Lord,

Proverbs 8:13

The fear of the Lord is to hate evil.

Why Doesn't God Just End All Suffering Now?

And yet, man's inhumanity to man continues. Why? It's because He has given mankind freewill, and He will not violate that. Even in the final judgment for unbelievers, God is respecting their right to choose their eternal destiny—eternal destruction. Christian philosopher, apologist and author, C.S. Lewis, put it this way:

There are only two kinds of people in the end: those who say to God, "Thy will be done," and those to whom God says, in the end, "Thy will be done." All that are in Hell, choose it. Without that self-choice there could be no Hell.[34]

Mankind has freewill. With freewill mankind can choose to love or hate; to lift people up or cause them agony. God will not force Himself on anyone. He is a Gentleman.

Question: Why doesn't God just end it all right now? The answer is two-fold.

First, God has a plan that He is executing.

Isaiah 46:9-11

For I am God, and there is no other; I am God, and there is no one like Me, declaring the end from the beginning, and from ancient times things which have not been done, saying, 'My purpose will be established, and I will accomplish all My good pleasure'. ... Truly I have spoken; truly I will bring it to pass. I have planned it, surely I will do it.

God has a plan, and this plan has a timetable. God has always had a timetable. Even Jesus was born at a specific time.

Galatians 4:4

But when the set time had fully come, God sent his Son, born of a woman.

God has a set time for everything in His plan, but that is for Him to know, not us. Not even Jesus knew the exact time of His second coming. When addressing the subject of the end times, Jesus made this statement:

Matthew 24:36

But of that day and hour no one knows, not even the angels of heaven, nor the Son, but the Father alone.

So first, God has a plan and that plan has a timetable.
The second reason that God hasn't just ended it all right now is mentioned in 2 Peter.

2 Peter 3:3-4,8-9

*But of that day and hour no one knows, not even the angels of heaven, nor the Son, but the Father alone. ... But do not let this one fact escape your notice, beloved, that with the Lord one day is like a thousand years, and a thousand years like one day. The Lord is not slow about His promise, as some count slowness, but **is patient toward you, not wishing for any to perish but for all to come to repentance**.*

Another reason God waits is because He is compassionate and patient with humanity, and doesn't wish anyone to perish. God desires more and more people to choose eternal life by choosing His Son, Jesus Christ.

We may yearn for God to end it all now, but I dare say all of us know family and friends that we love dearly who haven't become Christ-followers yet, and therefore don't have eternal life. That one thought should cause us to slow down on the "God just end it" sentiment.

CHAPTER 18

Because We're Doing Something Right

Sometimes suffering happens because we're doing something right, not something wrong! Suffering is triggered by going against the flow; by standing up for a cause, truth or righteousness. All one has to do is look at Jesus Christ, for He stood for all three; a cause, truth and righteousness.

A Cause

Anytime you stand up for a cause you can bank on persecution and suffering. History is replete with examples of this.

The supreme example is Jesus Christ Himself. He was light that penetrated a world of darkness, but the cause of light wasn't received well.

John 1:5

The Light shines in the darkness, and the darkness did not comprehend it.

We all know how that ended— a crucifixion. Anytime one stands up for a cause, persecution and suffering will be the inevitable result.

Englishman William Wilberforce (1759-1833), became a politician when he was twenty-one years old. When he was twenty-six years old, he became a Christian. One year later, Wilberforce launched into the cause for which he is still famous— the abolition of the slave trade. It was through this one man's campaign to end suffering that the slave trade in England eventually ended with the passing of the Abolition bill, February 23, 1807. The bill became the Slave Trade Act on March 25, 1807. In 1818 William Wilberforce wrote in his diary:

In the Scripture, no national crime is condemned so frequently and few so strongly as oppression and cruelty, and the not using our best endeavors to deliver our fellow-creatures from them.[35]

But make no mistake, Wilberforce suffered for leading this cause. One only needs to watch the 2006 movie, *Amazing Grace*, to see the persecution and contempt that Wilberforce endured.

William Tyndale (1494-1536) was strangled to death while tied to a stake, then his dead body burned, all for one reason…he translated the Bible into English. William Tyndale suffered for a cause—for doing something right.

A certain kind of cause is whistleblowing. All legitimate whistleblowers experience this kind of blowback and suffering.

- Norma Rae, portrayed by Sally Field, in the 1979 movie, *Norma Rae.*
- Karen Silkwood, portrayed by Meryl Streep, in the 1983, *Silkwood.*
- Jeffrey Wigand, a tobacco company executive, portrayed by Russell Crowe, in the 1999 movie, *The Insider.*
- Sherron Watkins, Vice President of Corporate Development at Enron, the whistleblower who helped expose the fraud of Enron and Kenneth Lay in 2002. Enron's demise is captured in the 2005 documentary, *Enron: The Smartest Guys in the Room.*

We could also cite the persecution and suffering endured by leaders of the women's suffrage movement of the late 1800s and early 1900s, along with Martin Luther King and other leaders of the 1960s civil rights movement.

These are examples of suffering because of doing something right, spearheading a noble cause.

Truth

Standing up for the truth will always cause suffering, whether on the world stage, at the office water cooler, or even at the kitchen table with family.

Jesus Christ spoke truth and suffered for it. The truth He preached riled up the religious world of His day. Although, for the most part, the common person embraced His message of grace and forgiveness, it didn't go over so well with the religious elite.

Jesus spoke the truth to the Pharisees and religious leaders. Notice the result.

John 8:54-59

*Jesus answered, "If I glorify Myself, My glory is nothing; it is My Father who glorifies Me, of whom you say, 'He is our God'; and you have not come to know Him, but I know Him; and if I say that I do not know Him, I will be a liar like you, but I do know Him and keep His word. Your father Abraham rejoiced to see My day, and he saw it and was glad." So the Jews said to Him, "You are not yet fifty years old, and have You seen Abraham?" Jesus said to them, "Truly, truly, I say to you, **before Abraham was born, I am**." Therefore they picked up stones to throw at Him, but Jesus hid Himself and went out of the temple.*

When Jesus said those words, "Before Abraham was born, I am," He was stating that He was in fact, God. It was a claim to deity. Remember when Moses asked God what His name was, which he needed to know when later speaking to the Israelites, God's answer was: "I AM." (Exodus 3:14)

When the Pharisees heard Jesus say He existed before Abraham and then use this sacred name for God, *I AM*, they went ballistic. The reason they picked up stones to stone Jesus was because of Leviticus 24:16, which states those guilty of blasphemy must be stoned to death. Except that Jesus wasn't committing blasphemy, He was speaking the truth. Speaking the truth is why Jesus came into the world.

John 18:37

For this I have been born, and for this I have come into the world, to testify to the truth. Everyone who is of the truth hears My voice.

Speaking the truth got John the Baptist executed. John was in prison, and told King Herod that he was living in adultery and needed to repent. It didn't go over so well. Herod had John the Baptist beheaded (refer to Matthew 14:1-12).

In 1 Kings 22, a prophet by the name Micaiah endured suffering because he didn't issue pleasant and encouraging words from God to the King of Israel. The King of Israel was accustomed to hearing nice prophecies from his four hundred yes-men prophets.

1 Kings 22:13

> *Then the messenger who went to summon Micaiah spoke to him saying, "Behold now, the words of the prophets are uniformly favorable to the king. Please let your word be like the word of one of them, and speak favorably."*

But when inquiring from Micaiah about whether Israel should go to war, Micaiah gave the king a word that he didn't want to hear.

1 Kings 22:23

> *The Lord has proclaimed disaster against you.*

For speaking the truth from God, Micaiah went to prison. One prophet spoke the truth, four hundred spoke falsehoods. When you're in the .0025% of people speaking truth, you can expect suffering.

Martin Luther (1483-1546), in confronting the religious system of his day and spearheading the Reformation, endured suffering for the rest of his life. Keep in mind that Jesus along with the Apostles and Paul died martyrs' deaths. Speaking truth is a risky thing, but we must do it.

One area of speaking truth that fascinates me, is in the area of *apologetics*, which is defense of the faith using good, sound reasoning. Those who promote Intelligent Design (ID) in the academic world face tremendous contempt from the scientific community. And yet, ID is based totally on science.

Many credentialed ID apologists with notable academic pedigrees are fired or demoted for suggesting that all scientific evidence points to an Intelligent Designer who created the universe. The 2008 movie, *Expelled: No Intelligence Allowed*, documents this contempt against IDers. Authors and researchers remotely connected to *The Discovery Institute* in Seattle, are shunned because they dare question a sacrosanct belief held in the scientific and academic communities—Darwinian evolution.

Righteousness

Standing up for righteousness or pointing out sin when appropriate will also cause suffering. As mentioned earlier, John the Baptist confronted Herod on his adultery and ended up being beheaded for it. William Wilberforce pointed out sin and suffered for it.

We are living in an interesting time in which political correctness rules. One dare not expose sin lest they incur the wrath of society. If one has the courage to say that something is sinful, like homosexuality, transgender, gay marriage or abortion, the immediate and blistering reaction from people is, "Who are you to say that's sinful? Judge not lest you be judged," which is a complete misinterpretation of Matthew 7:1. And yet, standing up for righteousness and exposing evil is commanded of us. For example, I believe we are to stand against abortion and stand for life.

Proverbs 31:8-9

Speak up for those who cannot speak for themselves; ensure justice for those being crushed. Yes, speak up for the poor and helpless, and see that they get justice.

I believe we are to stand against homosexuality, transgender and gay marriage, while standing up for God's design for sexuality and marriage. This of course, will incur the wrath of society. Yet, as Christians, we must speak up.

Ephesians 5:11

*Do not participate in the unfruitful deeds of darkness, **but instead even expose them**.*

Psalm 94:16

***Who will stand up for me against evildoers?** Who will take his stand for me against those who do wickedness?*

Titus 1:10,11

> *For there are many rebellious men, empty talkers and deceivers...**who must be silenced** because they are upsetting whole families, teaching things they should not teach.*

It takes courage to do this. Pointing out evil and sin shouldn't be our main focus, but at the same time, if the opportunity arises and the moment of truth comes, we shouldn't remain silent, we should speak the truth with grace and tact (Ephesians 4:15, Colossians 4:6). The reason we don't speak up is because we don't want to be persecuted or rejected. We want to be liked by everyone. Jesus had something to say about that.

Luke 6:26

> *Woe to you when all men speak well of you, for their fathers used to treat the false prophets in the same way.*

We read about false prophets earlier. They were well received by the king and his leaders. All men spoke well of the false prophets, but not of God's true prophet.

Targets

Whether we realize it or not, we are in a spiritual warfare.

Ephesians 6:12

> *For our struggle is not against flesh and blood, but against the rulers, against the powers, against the world forces of this darkness, against the spiritual forces of wickedness in the heavenly places.*

Question: Who are the first targets in battle? Answer: The ones sticking their heads up and actively DOING something! Those in the back working in the office don't get shot at. It's believers who are actively walking with God and holding forth His Word and modeling His character that get attacked, both by humans and the devil.

Philippians 2:16 says we should be "holding forth the word of life," not hiding it. When we hold forth the word of life, we become obvious.

It is those getting close to God and active in expanding God's kingdom that get persecuted, not the silent ones. The Apostle Paul was constantly attacked because he was dangerous to the kingdom of darkness!

When I first became a Christian, in the summer between my junior and senior year of high school, I experienced persecution and some suffering. I was ostracized by the gang I hung out with for being a Christian.

It was partly my fault because when I first became a Christ-follower, I was very bold and too "in your face." I probably should have been caged for six months until I learned Colossians 4:6, "Let your speech always be with grace, as though seasoned with salt." But I was a new Christian and on fire.

One immediate change in my life was that I no longer made fun of or put down people that weren't as 'cool' as us. I would even speak up and defend the one being picked on. I no longer got drunk with the gang (that came later in life, which my other book touched on).[36] That didn't go over so well, and eventually I was asked the leave the lunch table with the gang and sit somewhere else, and this was from close friends with whom I had hung out with since first and second grade.

Those relationships have all since been restored, but at the time, it was very difficult for me. "Woe to you when all men speak well of you."

Some suffering in this world occurs when we take a stand for a cause, the truth, or for righteousness. Some suffering happens, not because you're doing something wrong, but because you're doing something right!

CHAPTER 19

Because of Unwise or Downright Stupid Decisions

Suffering sometimes happens when we make unwise or downright stupid decisions. Because God created mankind with free will, and because man chooses to walk apart from common sense or wisdom, God should not be blamed for the inevitable bad consequences. One just needs to read, *The Darwin Awards[37]*, to appreciate this. With six books and its own website, evidently these awards continue to be bestowed upon people regularly.

The Bible is God's written revelation and instructions for mankind. Sometimes we like to refer to the Bible as our *Manufacturer's Handbook*. The operator's handbook for your car contains valuable information on how to operate the vehicle in the right manner, how to maintain it so it achieves optimal performance, and how to troubleshoot it when things go wrong.

The Bible does that for mankind. That's why God talks about gaining wisdom, understanding and discretion in many places, especially in the book of Proverbs.

Proverbs 4:5

Acquire wisdom! Acquire understanding! Do not forget nor turn away from the words of my mouth.

And where do we find this wisdom and understanding?

Proverbs 2:6

> *For the Lord gives wisdom; from His mouth come knowledge and understanding.*

What comes out of your mouth? Words. What comes out of God's mouth? Words. God's Word is the source of wisdom, knowledge and understanding.

Often people don't seriously contemplate the foolishness of what they're doing, and sadly, suffer the results for it. But this isn't rocket science—unwise or downright stupid decisions cost.

Proverbs 14:8 NIV

> *The wisdom of the prudent is to give thought to their ways, but the folly of fools is deception.*

The deception is when someone thinks, "I'll do this but I'm different, I'll be o.k." They find out otherwise.

It grieves my heart deeply when I read about girls who are murdered after walking home alone at night from a party or bar. How many girls have to be murdered before girls learn that they can't walk alone at night? Someone will argue, "But that shouldn't be the way it is, they should be able to walk home alone at night and not be bothered!" True, but living with wisdom dictates responding to reality in prudent ways. We shouldn't have to lock our doors at night, but we do because we meet reality with discretion and wisdom. Many times suffering happens when we discard wisdom, discretion and common sense.

- How many married couples will get divorced because they rang up way too much debt and their marriage buckled underneath the load?
- How many people will die because of texting and driving?
- How many adolescent children will go off the rails because parents failed to closely monitor where they went, what they did, and who their close friends were?
- How many people will die prematurely because of smoking?
- How many men and women's minds will be infected and sickened by pornography?
- How many married couples will get divorced because one of them didn't put in place some accountability

and safeguards to protect against extramarital relationships?
- How many young adults will waste their lives on things that don't matter instead of getting an education or acquiring a marketable skill?
- How many people have to overdose on drugs?

In each case, a lack of wisdom or foolish decisions were the root problem.

Proverbs 6:27-29 NLT

Can a man scoop a flame into his lap and not have his clothes catch on fire? Can he walk on hot coals and not blister his feet? So it is with the man who sleeps with another man's wife. He who embraces her will not go unpunished.

It's basically saying here, "Can you totally go against wisdom and expect good results?" No! Suffering will be the inevitable result. And when it happens, someone will cry out, "How could God do this to me?" He didn't!

Proverbs 19:3

The foolishness of man ruins his way, and his heart rages against the Lord.

Friend, it wasn't God, it was an unwise or downright stupid decision. Don't blame God for consequences of a foolish decision. Acquiring and operating with God's wisdom is the answer.

Proverbs 4:7 NLT

Getting wisdom is the wisest thing you can do! And whatever else you do, develop good judgment.

What is true for individuals is true for nations. When a nation doesn't act with wisdom regarding national debt or policies, they set themselves up for a financial collapse. This is what happened in September 2008 with the Wall Street market crash. When a nation thumbs their nose at God and embraces immorality, they set themselves up for a fall. And when the fall happens, the people who suffer will cry out, "How could God let this happen?" He let it happen because the country's leaders have free will and chose to make unwise or downright stupid decisions that opened the door for evil instead of closing it. All the while God was trying to get them to act with wisdom, but they spurned God's wisdom.

Proverbs 14:34

Righteousness exalts a nation, but sin is a disgrace to any people.

There are consequences for thumbing one's nose at God instead of embracing His wisdom.

Proverbs 1:20-33 NIV

20 *Out in the open wisdom calls aloud, she raises her voice in the public square;*

21 *on top of the wall she cries out, at the city gate she makes her speech:*

22 *"How long will you who are simple love your simple ways? How long will mockers delight in mockery and fools hate knowledge?*

23 *Repent at my rebuke! Then I will pour out my thoughts to you, I will make known to you my teachings.*

24 *But since you refuse to listen when I call and no one pays attention when I stretch out my hand,*

25 *since you disregard all my advice and do not accept my rebuke,*

26 *I in turn will laugh when disaster strikes you; I will mock when calamity overtakes you—*

27 *when calamity overtakes you like a storm, when disaster sweeps over you like a whirlwind, when distress and trouble overwhelm you.*

28 *"Then they will call to me but I will not answer; they will look for me but will not find me,*

29 *since they hated knowledge and did not choose to fear the Lord.*

> 30 *Since they would not accept my advice and spurned my rebuke,*
>
> 31 *they will eat the fruit of their ways and be filled with the fruit of their schemes.*
>
> 32 *For the waywardness of the simple will kill them, and the complacency of fools will destroy them;*
>
> 33 *but whoever listens to me will live in safety and be at ease, without fear of harm."*

At a certain point, God gives individuals and nations what they wanted. He allows them to "eat the fruit of their ways."

I repeat, God's Word is our *Manufacturer's Handbook*. Life turns out better when we conduct our lives in line with that handbook.

Christian psychologist and one of my favorite authors, Dr. Henry Cloud, names three kinds of people that the Bible identifies: The evil man, the foolish man, and the wise man. This 22-minute video is worth watching—https://vimeo.com/43777476[38]. The bottom line is, the wise man, when getting corrected will make adjustments. The foolish man just makes excuses and won't adjust what he's doing. It's always someone else's fault.

Proverbs 12:1

> *Whoever loves discipline loves knowledge, but he who hates reproof is stupid.*

I don't think we need to debate the interpretation of that, it's crystal clear.

Unfortunately, it's the citizens of a nation that suffer when their leaders make unwise or downright stupid decisions. The people of Germany (and the world) suffered because of the decisions of Kaiser Wilhelm II (World War I) and Hitler (World War II).

The same thing happens in families when children suffer in broken homes. 41% of births in the United States are outside of the context of marriage[39]. There are negative consequences to that.

Individuals and married couples suffer when they make unwise financial decisions. A married couple will purchase or build a house based on two incomes, not factoring in the absence of a spouse in the child bearing or rearing years; or, not having a financial buffer in case of loss of job or health. People also suffer when they get involved in dubious multilevel marketing schemes, losing money and friends. And when it happens they will cry out, "Why did God allow this to happen to me?" He allowed it because: 1) You have free will, and 2) You made unwise decisions.

Proverbs 13:11 NLT

Wealth from get-rich-quick schemes quickly disappears; wealth from hard work grows over time.

Suffering also happens when we make unwise decisions regarding our bodies and health. Diet, nutrition, exercise, rest, good dental and personal hygiene, and regular doctor and dentist visits are all important factors that prevent suffering. I struggle with regular exercise. My idea of exercise is filling the bathtub, jumping in, pulling the plug and fighting the current. That's just about all the excitement I can take. Yet I, along with many others, need to incorporate good diet and exercise to prevent future suffering. Again, it's this law of sowing and reaping.

1 Timothy 4:8 NLT

Physical training is good, but training for godliness is much better, promising benefits in this life and in the life to come."

Sometimes people suffer when they delay going to the doctor. Most of the time this happens with men. I remember hearing about a well-known pastor getting cancer and eventually dying. I was grieved over this because I knew this pastor believed in and preached divine health and healing. Years later I found out what really happened. When he first heard that he had cancer, he delayed radiation and chemo because he didn't want his congregation to know about it. That delay cost him his life. It was an unwise decision.

A lot of suffering can't be blamed on God, but happens when we make unwise or downright stupid decisions.

Proverbs 1:7

The fear of the LORD is the beginning of knowledge; fools despise wisdom and instruction.

Proverbs 27:12 NIV

The prudent see danger and take refuge, but the simple keep going and pay the penalty.

CHAPTER 20

10

Because of Reasons We'll Never Know
This Side of Eternity

Why is there suffering?

1. Because we live in a fallen world.
2. Because of 'already but not yet'.
3. Because it's a direct attack from Satan.
4. Because we're actively living in sin.
5. Because we're living outside of God's will.
6. Because we haven't appropriated God's blessings.
7. Because of man's inhumanity to man.
8. Because we're doing something right.
9. Because of unwise or downright stupid decisions.

One problem with a list like this is, although helpful, it may cause people angst because they can't quite put their finger on a reason and consequently, feel guilty and condemned. They may even ascribe their suffering to one of these reasons that is not even valid in their case. That's unfortunate because I want the list to bring light, not confusion.

The truth is...many times bad things happen to good people, and we have absolutely no idea why. Almost all of us know someone who died prematurely or experienced great suffering because of an illness or disability. It's normal to ask "why", we do that instinctively. But when all is said and done, we may never know the 'why'.

My brother, John, died suddenly and unexpectedly, Saturday evening, December 1, 2001, of a heart attack at the age of 47. He was one year younger than me, and we were very close. His death sent me into an emotional tailspin. I wrote about this in my book, *The Pastor and the Prayer*[40]. Even though I knew that God didn't cause his death, I was still mad at God that it happened, and none of us knew why.

For three years I battled depression and was suicidal. I began to get weekly counseling from a Christian psychologist. For an entire year he worked with me, trying to get me to the place that I could accept and live with this truth: *Life is unfair and always will be.*

I couldn't accept that truth because I lived in a world of "should," "must" and "ought," along with their opposites; "should not," "must not," and "ought not". My brother "should not" have died.

My brother had no prior heart problems, he jogged almost daily, played competitive soccer, and refereed high school soccer games. He was in great shape, and then, in an instant, died. That's not fair. When I prayed and asked God "why," heaven was silent. Heaven continued to be silent.

After several years of this, still banging on heaven's door for an answer, God led me to Deuteronomy 29:29.

Deuteronomy 29:29

The secret things belong to the LORD our God, but the things revealed belong to us and to our children forever.

This is what God was saying to me: "Tom, sometimes I reveal why something bad happened, and when I do, it's for you to know and be helped by. But there are other times when I don't reveal it to you. When that happens, it's a secret thing that only belongs to Me, and you should leave it alone."

In fact, God told me that to "demand" that He tell me the reason why something bad happened was a form of control and manipulation, something He didn't much appreciate.

If we don't understand why, if it's not revealed to us, then it's a secret thing that belongs to the Lord, and we should leave it alone in our thought life, and continue to follow and trust God.

Demanding to know a secret thing that only belongs to God will cause us harm through anger, depression or creating distance between ourselves and God. In these cases, we must trust God and continue to live in peace, knowing that God will make all things right in the end.

Most people are familiar with the first stanza of *The Serenity Prayer*, but very few have read the entire prayer. Here it is:

The Serenity Prayer

God, grant me the serenity to accept the things I
cannot change,
The courage to change the things I can,
And the wisdom to know the difference.

Living one day at a time, enjoying one moment at a
time;
Accepting hardship as a pathway to peace,

Taking as Jesus did, this sinful world as it is, not as I
would have it;
Trusting that You will make all things right if I
surrender to Your will;

So that I may be reasonably happy in this life,
And supremely happy with You forever in the next.
Amen.

Without exaggeration—understanding, praying and living out this prayer saved my life. It's the subject of my book mentioned earlier, *The Pastor and the Prayer*. I clung to that line, "Trusting that You will make all things right if I surrender to Your will."

At the end of the day, when suffering happens and we don't know why, we must leave it alone in our thought life and trust God to make all things right as we surrender to His will for our lives.

One thing I've learned about suffering in my own life, is the truth of 2 Corinthians 1:3,4.

2 Corinthians 1:3-4

Blessed be the God and Father of our Lord Jesus Christ, the Father of mercies and God of all comfort, who comforts us in all our affliction so that we will be able to comfort those who are in any affliction with the comfort with which we ourselves are comforted by God!

As a result of my suffering with the loss of my brother, I am in a better place to comfort those who experience similar things.

Like me, you may never know the reason for the suffering you or a loved one has experienced. If it's not revealed to you, then let God have it as a secret thing that belongs only to Him, and then live in peace as you trust Him to make all things right as you surrender to His will.

Chapter 21

Suffering vs. Triumphalism

I will be accused, no doubt, of promoting a theology called "triumphalism." *Triumphalism* is the theology that we will always triumph in this life and never experience failure, defeat or suffering of any kind.

Sometimes this theology is called "over-realized eschatology." "Eschatology" means what happens in the future, and "over-realized" means expecting to realize or experience something one has no right to experience right now. So "over-realized eschatology" is expecting to experience now what will only be experienced in heaven. It is a theology that says that we will experience in totality now, all the blessings afforded us in the age to come.

This view comes from certain verses, for example, 2 Corinthians 2:14.

2 Corinthians 2:14

> *But thanks be to God, who **always** leads us in triumph in Christ, and manifests through us the sweet aroma of the knowledge of Him in every place.*

At first glance, this seems to support the idea that we will never experience suffering or adversity, but ALWAYS victory. Let me share two important points about this verse.

First, the context of the verse is God leading us in triumph as we take this gospel of Jesus Christ to the world ("the knowledge of Him in every place"). In this context, we will ALWAYS triumph because even if people don't receive the gospel, we obeyed God in sharing it (along with living it out before people).

Second, the verse does not say we will never suffer on this earth, it says God will lead us to triumph. We will suffer, but we can triumph. We could just as easily interpret the verse like Romans 8:28.

Romans 8:28

And we know that God causes all things to work together for good to those who love God, to those who are called according to His purpose.

He doesn't cause all things, He causes all things to work together for the good! In the same vein, 2 Corinthians 2:14 doesn't mean we'll never suffer, but that God will lead us to triumph, especially as it concerns taking the knowledge of God to every place our feet carry us.

We have a continuum with polar-opposite ends. We have suffering (allegedly that it's God's will that we suffer) on one end of the continuum, and triumphalism (allegedly that we will always triumph and never experience suffering) on the other end of the continuum. Both are ditches to be avoided!

Truth be told, we will experience adversity on this earth, regardless of whether we're living for the Lord or not. Jesus talked about this. The storms of adversity hit the believer and unbeliever alike.

Luke 6:47-49

47 Everyone who comes to Me and hears My words and acts on them, I will show you whom he is like:

48 he is like a man building a house, who dug deep and laid a foundation on the rock; and when a __flood__ occurred, the __torrent__ burst against that house and could not shake it, because it had been well built.

49 But the one who has heard and has not acted accordingly, is like a man who built a house on the ground without any foundation; and the __torrent__ burst against it and immediately it collapsed, and the ruin of that house was great."

We have two kinds of people mentioned here, the person who built his house with no foundation (hearing God's Word but not acting on it, e.g., disobedience), and the other who dug deep and built his house on a firm foundation of rock (hearing and acting on God's Word, e.g., obedience).

What is noteworthy here is that the person who heard the Word of God and acted on it STILL experienced the same flood and storm as the person who heard God's Word and didn't act on it. The difference was that the person who laid the foundation by hearing and obeying God's Word triumphed, while the other person experienced complete ruin.

So I am not advocating for the ditch of triumphalism. Just understanding the first two reasons for human suffering (we're living in a fallen world, and 'the already but not yet') will account for the reality of a certain degree of suffering for ALL of us. The only thing you have to do to experience suffering is to be born. Period.

Yet, God's will is still healing, which I believe was provided for us in the atonement (what Jesus accomplished for us at the cross). And I believe God's will is to heal all.

Acts 10:38

> *You know of Jesus of Nazareth, how God anointed Him with the Holy Spirit and with power, and how He went about doing good and healing **all** who were oppressed by the devil, for God was with Him.*

Matthew 9:35 NIV

> *Jesus went through all the towns and villages, teaching in their synagogues, proclaiming the good news of the kingdom and healing **every** disease and sickness.*

And even though I believe God's will is healing for all...I still have to face the fact that some will never be healed. That's the mystery of the "already but not yet". It's a *mystery* for a good reason—we don't fully understand it.

There are people afflicted with severe disabilities that will never be healed this side of heaven. We must accept this reality. There are blind people who are healed, but most aren't. There are deaf people healed, but most aren't. I have never heard of a paraplegic being healed, nor someone with severe cerebral palsy or Down Syndrome. That doesn't preclude God from working a miracle by healing these infirmities, it just means we're living in the reality of the 'already but not yet'. But that should not deter us from praying for healing.

Question: How does one pastor a church holding to a theology of triumphalism? Answer: You can't! Your people will see the disparity between their lives and your theology of triumphalism and dismiss both it and you. Or...they will buy into it and then experience tremendous conflict and guilt when they experience suffering. The better option for pastors and teachers is to tell the truth by affirming God's will to heal and deliver, but simultaneously explaining three of the ten reasons for suffering:

1. We live in a fallen world.
2. Already but not yet.
3. There are reasons we'll never know on this side of eternity.

To go beyond this is to flirt with the warped theology of the disciples in John 9. "Rabbi, who sinned that this man was born blind—the man or his parents?" Jesus' response? "Neither!"

All of us will experience suffering to some degree, that's just reality. But there are some steps we can take in the midst of suffering.

Dealing with Suffering

There is a danger in listing steps as a solution. Doing so tends to make it seem too easy (just follow these steps and your problem is solved), and additionally, it may exclude a critical step not thought of. But risking this danger, I still think it prudent to show some ways to biblically respond to suffering.

Step 1 – Trust

James 1:13

Is anyone among you suffering? Then he must pray.

This is our number one response while experiencing suffering. We must pray and affirm our trust in God that He will take care of us.

1 Peter 5:7

Casting all your anxiety on Him, because He cares for you.

Psalm 55:22

Cast your burden upon the Lord and He will sustain you;

When suffering, we must cast our cares and burdens upon the Lord, declaring our unwavering trust for His help and guidance. Although Job was wrong in believing that God was the one making him suffer, I still love how in the middle of his suffering, he gave himself to God in complete trust.

Job 13:15

Though He slay me, I will hope in Him.

We must stay hooked up to God in complete trust, even when things are going wrong.

John 14:1

Do not let your heart be troubled; believe in God, believe also in Me.

If this is new to you, or you're having problems trusting God, I encourage you to read Parts 2 and 3 of my book *The Pastor and the Prayer*.

Step 2 – Joy and Peace

Trusting God, I mean TRULY trusting God, will produce something...joy and peace.

Romans 15:13 NIV

*I pray that God, the source of hope, will fill you completely with **joy and peace because you trust in him**. Then you will overflow with confident hope through the power of the Holy Spirit.*

Joy and peace are the offspring of trust. In the midst of suffering, keep your joy and peace while trusting.

James 1:2-4

> *Consider it all joy, my brethren, when you encounter various trials, knowing that the testing of your faith produces endurance. And let endurance have its perfect result, so that you may be perfect and complete, lacking in nothing.*

Step 3 – The Prayer of Faith

One of the ten reasons for suffering was that we didn't appropriate God's promises of healing, provision, or guidance through the prayer of faith. We didn't put up the shield of faith. James 4:2 says, "You have not because you ask not."

At some point, we must get quiet before the Lord and pray in faith for healing, provision, or deliverance from oppression.

James 5:14,15

> *Is anyone among you sick? Then he must call for the elders of the church and they are to pray over him, anointing him with oil in the name of the Lord; and the prayer offered in faith will restore the one who is sick, and the Lord will raise him up, and if he has committed sins, they will be forgiven him.*

Pray in faith for God's healing, provision, strength, comfort and guidance.

Step 4 – Ask for Wisdom

In the middle of suffering we all experience the same conundrum...what are we supposed to do?

No matter what we're suffering, we should ask God for wisdom on how to handle the situation. Immediately after verses 2 to 4 which deal with facing various trials, we find verses 5 and 6.

James 1:5-6

> *But if any of you lacks wisdom, let him ask of God, who gives to all generously and without reproach, and it will be given to him. But he must ask in faith without any doubting.*

In the context of suffering various trials, here we are seeking wisdom and guidance from God, both on what may have caused the suffering (if anything), and what we should do now.

Is this because I'm outside of God will? Is this because I'm living in sin? Is this because I've made unwise or downright stupid decisions? If none of those things, God, what would You have me to do now? Is there someone You would have me counsel with about this?

By the mere fact that we are instructed to ask for wisdom proves that we don't automatically have it. So ask for it.

Step 5 – If appropriate, repentance followed by good decisions

Sometimes (and I stress here, not all the time), suffering is caused by foolish decisions, living outside of God will for our lives, or downright intentionally living in sin. If this has been the case, we should repent and return to the Lord.

1 John 1:9

If we confess our sins, He is faithful and righteous to forgive us our sins and to cleanse us from all unrighteousness.

There are three important elements to repentance:

1. Godly sorrow.

2 Corinthians 7:9 – "I now rejoice, not that you were made sorrowful, but that you were made sorrowful to the point of repentance; for you were made sorrowful according to the will of God."

2. Confession of the sin before God.

Psalm 32:5 – "I acknowledged my sin to You, and my iniquity I did not hide."

3. A change of direction.

Matthew 3:8 NLT – "Prove by the way you live that you have repented of your sins and turned to God." For a more detailed treatment of repentance I refer you to my book *Lord and Savior*.

Step 6 – Actively resist Satan

Some, not all, of suffering continues because we don't take an active step to resist Satan, the one causing it. But we are told in Scripture to actively resist Satan and his activities.

James 4:7

__Resist__ the devil and he will flee from you.

1 Peter 5:8-9

Be of sober spirit, be on the alert. Your adversary, the devil, prowls around like a roaring lion, seeking someone to devour. But __resist__ him, firm in your faith.

Ephesians 6:16

__Taking up the shield of faith__ with which you will be able __to extinguish__ all the flaming arrows of the evil one.

Luke 9:1

And He called the twelve together, and gave them __power and authority over all the demons__ and to heal diseases.

Don't ask God to do it, you do it. He's already given us authority to use the name of Jesus to resist and rebuke Satan. "Satan, I rebuke and resist what you are doing in my life and command that you cease and desist your activity right now. Be gone from me now, in Jesus' name."

Step 7 – Incorporate the force of endurance

Remember the two important things we learned from the book of Job: trust and endurance. Patience (or endurance), is a spiritual force given to us by the Holy Spirit. If we have crossed the line of faith and have become Christ-followers, patience already resides within us (Galatians 5:22, the fruit of the Spirit is—patience). But we must express this fruit of the Spirit.

Hebrews 6:12

That you will not be sluggish, but imitators of those who __through faith and patience inherit the promises__.

Hebrews 10:36

> **For you have need of endurance**, *so that when you have done the will of God, you may receive what was promised.*

Like joy and peace, the key to experiencing endurance is trust. I can endure when I trust that God will strengthen me and bring good out of a bad situation.

I love the line from the full Serenity Prayer: "Taking as Jesus did, this sinful world as it is, not as I would have it, trusting that He will make all things right if I surrender to His will." Eventually, we must come to the place of trust, and when we do, we will endure.

Step 8 – Acceptance

The first part of the Serenity Prayer says: "God, grant me serenity **to accept** the things I cannot change, courage to change the things I can, and the wisdom to know the difference." Since 2009, I have been living that prayer daily (sometimes hourly).

There are things we can change and must have the courage to do so, incorporating some of the steps we've talked about (resisting the devil, the prayer of faith, getting back into the will of God, making good decisions, and appropriating God's blessings, etc.).

There are other things that will not change on this side of eternity. Things like permanent disabilities are forms of suffering that, unfortunately, won't change until we receive brand new bodies in the age to come. If this is the case, what is needed most is acceptance, and I would encourage you to read chapter 11 of my book, *The Pastor and the Prayer*. The chapter is entitled, *Serenity to Accept the Things I Cannot Change*. Space doesn't allow me to go into detail here, but acceptance for things we can't change brings peace.

If experiencing a permanent disability or a situation that, in all reality, can't be changed, although difficult, acceptance is the answer, for it will bring peace. And acceptance is based on trust in God.

In a church where I was pastoring, there was a man who had become paralyzed from the waist down because of wrong treatment he received for a heart ailment. What the doctors thought was a heart attack, really wasn't. This happened before I had come to the church to be their pastor. This man was angry, as you can imagine. But his anger wasn't just directed at the doctors who misdiagnosed him, it was toward God, his wife, his child, and the world in general.

I spent quite a bit of time counseling with him and directing him toward two of his most critical needs: forgiveness and acceptance. But he would not. Consequently, he never experienced peace and joy, all because he would not experience serenity by accepting the things he could not change. Acceptance was the elusive answer.

1 Timothy 6:6-8

But godliness actually is a means of great gain when accompanied by **contentment***. For we have brought nothing into the world, so we cannot take anything out of it either. If we have food and covering, with these we shall be* **content***.*

Trust in God will produce peace, joy and contentment (acceptance).

No, I am not advocating for triumphalism that says we'll never suffer in this life. But I do believe God still heals and delivers today and I make no apologies for that. At the same time, all of us will suffer in some way and in some degree. Some suffering we'll be delivered from, and some we will not. And for that suffering, trust and acceptance is God's way for us.

Finally, in dealing with suffering, we must adjust our thinking and our view of God and see Him how He really is. He is compassionate, and He relates to our suffering and wants "in" to our lives to help.

Isaiah 63:9

In all their suffering he also suffered, *and he personally rescued them. In his love and mercy he redeemed them. He lifted them up and carried them through all the years.*

God is not your problem, He is your answer.

Psalm 46:1

God is our refuge and strength, always ready to help in times of trouble.

And it's important to understand that Jesus knows what we're suffering and that He is there to comfort and strengthen us.

Hebrews 13:5

I will never fail you. I will never abandon you.

Hebrews 4:15

For we do not have a high priest who is unable to empathize with our weaknesses, *but we have one who has been tempted in every way, just as we are--yet he did not sin.*

Jesus was all God and all man at the same time. As a man living on this earth, He suffered. He experienced ridicule, rejection, torture and the eventual barbaric death of the cross. Jesus grieved over the loss of a loved one. The shortest verse in the Bible is just two words, "Jesus wept" (John 11:35). That was when His good friend Lazarus died. Jesus knows about loss and grief. God the Father knows about loss and grief...He lost His own beloved Son on the cross. If we will just come to God in prayer and pour out our heart to Him, He will meet us.

Psalm 145:18

The LORD is close to all who call on him, yes, to all who call on him in truth.

In the midst of our suffering, we must call upon Him, for He is called "the God of all comfort" (2 Corinthians 1:3).

Step 9 – Seek out help and support

Don't remain quiet or isolated, talk to someone, seek out the care and support you need to help you endure. It is a strange thing, but when suffering, many people prefer to withdraw and be quiet. I've experienced this myself more times than I care to admit. And although it may seem natural to withdraw, it is the worst thing you could possibly do, and for more than one reason.

First, everyone who suffers needs love, care and support. We're not made to suffer alone in isolation.

Ecclesiastes 4:9- 10 NLT

> *Two people are better off than one, for they can help each other succeed. If one person falls, the other can reach out and help. But someone who falls alone is in real trouble.*

Second, by keeping quiet, you rob people of the privilege of coming along side you and providing that support. People WANT to show care and support, but ONLY IF THEY KNOW ABOUT IT.

As a pastor, it used to frustrate me when our church would be criticized for not reaching out to someone who had suffered in some way. But truth be told...we never knew about it. Everyone assumed the church had been informed. Such was not the case. The one suffering needs to initiate contact with church leadership so that they can pray and offer help. I see this principle in James 5:14.

James 5:14, 15

> *Is anyone among you sick? Then **he must call for the elders of the church** and they are to pray over him, anointing him with oil in the name of the Lord; and the prayer offered in faith will restore the one who is sick, and the Lord will raise him up, and if he has committed sins, they will be forgiven him.*

The principle I see here is, if you're suffering, initiate contact with church leadership. They can't pray for or help you unless they know about it, and it's up to you to make the call. But this leads to looking at the flip side of the coin.

A Word to the Greater Faith Community

I would be remiss if I didn't touch on the role of churches, ministries, and the greater faith community in ministering to those who are suffering. What makes the sufferer feel even worse is when they feel isolated and/or unsupported.

We see this kind of **unsupported** experience of suffering with David, when hiding in a cave, fleeing from Saul who was trying to kill him.

Psalm 142:1-4 NLT

> *I cry out to the Lord; I plead for the Lord's mercy. I pour out my complaints before him and tell him all my troubles. When I am*

*overwhelmed, you alone know the way I should turn. Wherever I go, my enemies have set traps for me. I look for someone to come and help me, but no one gives me a passing thought! **No one will help me; no one cares a bit what happens to me**.*

I think we've all been there at one time or another. Suffering while feeling isolated, with no one really understanding what we're going through, has to be the worst. If we were to measure emotional pain from 1 to 10 with 10 being the greatest, suffering that would normally feel like a 10 might very well feel like a 5 when a person is tied into a network of support from family, friends, prayer partners and a faith community.

We are called by God to intentionally reach out in love and care for those we know who are suffering.

Romans 12:15

*Rejoice with those who rejoice, and **weep with those who weep**.*

Hebrews 6:10-11 NLT

*For God is not unjust. He will not forget how hard you have worked for him and **how you have shown your love to him by caring for other believers**, as you still do. Our great desire is that you will **keep on loving others as long as life lasts**, in order to make certain that what you hope for will come true.*

1 Corinthians 12:25

*That there may be no division in the body, but **that the members may have the same care for one another**.*

Romans 15:1-2

*Now **we who are strong ought to bear the weaknesses of those without strength** and not just please ourselves. Each of us is to please his neighbor for his good, to his edification.*

Galatians 6:2 NIV

> ***Carry each other's burdens***, *and in this way you will fulfill the law of Christ.*

James 1:27

> *Pure and undefiled religion in the sight of our God and Father is this:* **to visit orphans and widows in their distress**, *and to keep oneself unstained by the world.*

I believe we catch the spirit of the verse by thinking of *orphans* and *widows* as anyone who is suffering. Pure and genuine religion is reaching out to ANYONE who is suffering and needs care. The biggest mistake that most people make, including church leadership, is assuming that such support and care is being rendered. It is much better to be proactive and make contact to offer support. Don't assume it's been done.

Our response to suffering should be the same as Jesus' response. Remember what we saw from the story of the blind man in John 9. The disciples asked Jesus, "Who sinned, this man or his parents?" Jesus settled that quickly, my paraphrase: "Neither! Now let's get busy alleviating his suffering." And so it is with the response from the faith community…"How can we help?"

CHAPTER 22

Oh, What a Day That Will Be!

When I first became a Christian, I got turned onto the music of contemporary Christian artist Phil Keaggy. On his first Christian album, *What A Day*, he had a song by that same name. The song is about the day when we're all finally home together in heaven with the Lord. Here's verse 2:

> When we get Home, our Eternal Home
> There'll be no more sick and dying.
> No one is sad, no one is alone
> And there will be no more crying.
> He will wipe away every tear
> From His children's eyes
> And put a smile upon their faces.
> What a happy day when we see
> Our Lord in Paradise
> Crowned as King of Kings.
> What a day that will be
> Oh what a day that will be![41]

I loved that song then, and I love it just as much now. The day it speaks about is real, not fantasy.

Revelation 21:1-4

Then I saw a new heaven and a new earth; for the first heaven and the first earth passed away, and there is no longer any sea. And I saw the holy city, new Jerusalem, coming down out of heaven from God, made ready as a bride adorned for her husband. And I heard a loud voice from the throne, saying, "Behold, the tabernacle of God is among men, and He

> *will dwell among them, and they shall be His people, and God Himself will be among them, and He will wipe away every tear from their eyes; and there will no longer be any death; there will no longer be any mourning, or crying, or pain; the first things have passed away."*

Oh, what a day that will be!

All suffering will end on that day. Actually, all suffering has already ended for those Christ-followers who have died previously. They are in Paradise having been totally set free from sickness, pain, disability and sorrow. I don't care how good your day is going, their day today is exponentially better.

The day talked about in Revelation 21 is the day when Satan is finally banished forever, never more to tempt or afflict. It is the day when we get new physical bodies and live on a brand new physical earth in God's presence.

In this final state of heaven, where Christ-followers will enjoy eternal life, there will no longer be any sickness, disease, pain, disability, sorrow, death, oppression, sin, lack, or hatred. Why? Because there will no longer be any lingering vestiges of the curse, the curse brought on by Adam and Eve's sin.

Revelation 22:3

> *There will no longer be any curse.*

Without Satan or the curse, all suffering will be gone forever. I realize that that seems unreal and fuzzy to us now. Scripture says that at the present time we don't see things clearly.

1 Corinthians 13:12 NLT

> *Now we see things imperfectly, like puzzling reflections in a mirror, but then we will see everything with perfect clarity.*

Although it seems unreal, there's coming a day when all the grief, sorrow and suffering will be over for good.

And, we must remember that our eighty or ninety years here on earth seems like it will never end, but in reality, compared to eternity, it is a drop in the proverbial timeline bucket.

Romans 8:18

I consider that the sufferings of this present time are not worthy to be compared with the glory that is to be revealed to us.

2 Corinthians 4:17 NLT

For our present troubles are small and won't last very long. Yet they produce for us a glory that vastly outweighs them and will last forever!

Francis Chan does a great illustration with a rope representing life's timeline.[42] We must imagine that one end of the rope goes on forever, but the end that Francis Chan holds in his hands has about six inches that are painted red, the part that represents your life here on earth.

Francis Chan uses this to make a profound point: that six painted inches of rope, that eighty to ninety years of our earthly lives, determines what we will experience for eternity. Chan focuses in on how we spend our time and money during this time on earth, but I want to apply it to whatever degree of suffering we experience.

Whatever length of life we end up having and whatever degree of suffering we endure, it is nothing compared to the joy we'll experience in heaven for eternity.

James 4:14

You are just a vapor that appears for a little while and then vanishes away.

Notice the vapor coming off a kettle of boiling water on the stove...it disappears in a second. That's about how long our lives are in relation to eternity. And what we experience in heaven will absolutely eclipse anything we've experienced down here on earth. What things will we experience there? The Apostle Paul's answer:

1 Corinthians 2:9

Things which eye has not seen and ear has not heard, and which have not entered the heart of man, all that God has prepared for those who love Him.

Oh, what a day that will be.

About the Author

Tom Peers has served in ministry as a pastor and teacher since 1979.Tom, and wife Debby, pioneered a church in Rochester, New York, where Tom served as Senior Pastor for nineteen years. Tom has also served as Discipleship Pastor in Boynton Beach, Florida; Director of Operations for a ministry in Phoenix, Arizona; Executive Pastor for a church in Florence, Kentucky; Teaching Pastor at a church near Portland, Maine; and Senior Pastor in Portsmouth, New Hampshire.

Tom also served as a certified church consultant with Natural Church Development (NCD), certified Church Health Survey consultant under Dr. Thom Rainer, and strategic planning consultant with Leadership Development Resources (LDR) under Dr. Mel Ming.

Tom and Debby reside in Portland, Maine. They
have two grown children; Jesse (Rochester, New York) and Carissa (Houston, Texas).

Books by Tom Peers

The Pastor and the Prayer
Addiction Recovery Through Living the Serenity Prayer

How to be a Prime Target
We're All Targets – Some Make Better Targets Than Others

Fit, Function and Flourish
Your Place and Function in the Local Church

Lord and Savior
A Savior to be Received From – A Lord to be Obeyed

Is God to Blame?
Reconciling Suffering with a Good God

Faith Plus Faithfulness
A Biblical Response to *Once-Saved-Always-Saved*

Oil Upon My Head
The Importance of Correction in Spiritual Growth

EndNotes

1. Alvin Plantiga, Warranted Christian Belief, Oxford University Press, 2000, Pg 191
2. John R. Stott, The Cross of Christ, InterVarsity, 1986
3. https://en.wikiquote.org/wiki/The_Witches_of_East-wick_(film)
4. http://www.azquotes.com/quote/1038968
5. http://www.goodreads.com/quotes/8199-is-god-willing-to-pre-vent-evil-but-not-able-then
6. http://www.christianpost.com/news/im-probably-an-atheist-i-dont-buy-it-i-think-the-only-reason-for-religion-is-death-says-broadcaster-larry-king-134594/
7. http://www.nationalreview.com/article/205878/god-bless-ted-turner-rod-dreher
8. http://www.progressive.org/node/281
9. http://a.co/giCIaAj
10. What if Jesus Had Never Been Born - James Kennedy - Page 225
11. http://www.evolu-tionnews.org/2015/07/you_have_to_be097421.html
12. DVD series "Does God Exist?" – Session 9 – Dr. Stephen Myer – TrueU University (division of Focus on the Family)
13. Richard Dawkins, River Out of Eden, (New York: Basic Books, 1996), 133
14. FrankTurek, Stealing from God, (NavPress, 2014, 92)
15. Cornelius Van Til, A Christian Apologetic For Christian Apologists, p 56
16. Francis Beckwith and Gregory Koukl, *Relativism: Feet Firmly Planted in Mid-Air*, Baker Books, 1998
17. DVD series "Does God Exist?" – Session 10 – Dr. Stephen Myer – TrueU University (division of Focus on the Family)
18. Norman L. Geisler and Daniel J. McCoy, The Atheist's Fatal Flaw, Baker Books, 2014, p 112
19. http://www.brainyquote.com/quotes/quotes/v/vol-taire109646.html
20. Norman Geisler, Part 1 'Why I am Not a Five Point Calvinist,' https://www.youtube.com/watch?v=d9n_NU-oslp0&list=PLDFD2E37589EA81B9, Norman Geisler, 3:20

21   John MacArthur -
      https://www.youtube.com/watch?v=6LFzk1afiD8 (at 20:00)
22   http://www.christianquotes.info/quotes-by-author/john-wes-
      ley-quotes/
23   http://www.truthortradition.com/articles/who-sinned-that-this-
      man-was-born-blind
24   Greg Boyd, *God at War*, pg 233
25   https://www.youtube.com/watch?v=AKx-iJG5qrE – Starting
      at 5:45
26   https://www.Biblegateway.com/resources/matthew-
      henry/2Cor.12.1-2Cor.12.10
27   This thought comes from the book by Tom Tompkins, "Un-
      derstanding the Book of Job – Separating What is True From
      What is Truth"; Winlight Ministries, 2010; Kindle location
      276ff
28   In context, John 10:10 is referring to false teachers and messi-
      ahs. But the spiritual power behind them is Satan, the main
      spiritual culprit who steals, kills and destroys and inspires oth-
      ers to do so. John 8:44 – "You are of your father the devil, and
      you want to do the desires of your father. He was a murderer
      from the beginning, and does not stand in the truth because
      there is no truth in him. Whenever he speaks a lie, he speaks
      from his own nature, for he is a liar and the father of lies." The
      point there is that people may be murdering and lying, but it's
      the devil who is the father of all lying and murdering. The
      same thing applies with stealing, killing and destroying. If
      that's going on, it's the devil who is behind it. The exception
      to this is when God has used these things as divine judgment
      for wickedness.
29   Wired for Intimacy: How Pornography Hijacks the Male
      Brain; William M. Struthers, InterVarsity Press, 2010
30   Hyper-Grace, Michael L. Brown, Charisma House, 2014,
      http://amzn.to/2iGaQcN. Here, Dr. Brown does a wonderful
      job correcting the aberrant theology of the hyper-grace advo-
      cates.
31   https://www.blueletterbible.org/lang/lexicon/lexi-
      con.cfm?Strongs=G4318&t=KJV
32   https://en.wikipedia.org/wiki/List_of_geno-
      cides_by_death_toll
33   http://ow.ly/bjAQ305G3d5
34   C.S. Lewis, The Great Divorce
35   https://christianhistoryinstitute.org/magazine/article/william-
      wilberforce-did-you-know

[36] Tom Peers, The Pastor and the Prayer, Addiction Recovery Through Living the Serenity Prayer, Ragamuffin Publishing, 2015

[37] Wendy Northcutt, *The Darwin Awards*, Dutton Adult, 2000

[38] Henry Cloud video: https://vimeo.com/43777476

[39] http://www.foxnews.com/opinion/2012/07/22/psychological-impact-single-parenting.html

[40] Tom Peers, The Pastor and the Prayer, Addiction Recovery Through Living the Serenity Prayer, Ragamuffin Publishing, 2015

[41] http://lyrics.wikia.com/wiki/Phil_Keaggy:What_A_Day

[42] Francis Chan rope illustration (5:43 long): https://www.youtube.com/watch?v=jF_x8dsvb_4